THE MAKING *of*
HANDEL'S
Messiah

THE MAKING *of* HANDEL'S *Messiah*

ANDREW GANT

Bodleian Library
UNIVERSITY OF OXFORD

A NOTE ON DATES

Confusingly, Britain changed from the Julian to the Gregorian calendar right in the middle of the period covered by this narrative, in two stages between 1751 and 1752. Under the old system the legal New Year began on 25 March, so that for example December 1740 was followed by January 1740, up to 24 March 1740, then 25 March 1741. In this text I have adopted the tried and tested system of 'dual dating' for dates which fall between 1 January and 24 March under the old calendar, so that in the example above December 1740 is followed by January 1740/1, etc. until 25 March 1741. I hope the reader will thus be spared the 'divers inconveniences' and 'frequent mistakes in the dates of deeds and other writings' identified by Lord Chesterfield in his highly sensible Calendar (New Style) Act of 1750, which introduced the change.

First published in 2020 by the Bodleian Library
Broad Street, Oxford OX1 3BG
www.bodleianshop.co.uk

ISBN: 978 1 85124 506 2

Text © Andrew Gant 2020
All images © Bodleian Library, University of Oxford, 2020, unless specified on p.142

Andrew Gant has asserted his right to be identified as the author of this work.

Cover design by Dot Little at the Bodleian Library
Designed and typeset by Laura Parker in 9.8 on 15.8 Andulka Book Pro
Printed and bound by Toppan Leefung, China, on 157gsm Oji Zun Ma matt art paper

MIX
Paper from responsible sources
FSC® C104723
FSC www.fsc.org

British Library Catalogue in Publishing Data
A CIP record of this publication is available from the British Library

CONTENTS

INTRODUCTION

Messiah was born in two cities.

Something of eighteenth-century London survives in the streets and squares of Mayfair, where Handel lived and worked. Stroll along Brook Street, past the handsome red-brick facade of no. 25, where he composed the music of *Messiah* in the late summer of 1741, and you can catch its elegant echo in the broad avenues, generous street plans and tree-lined squares glimpsed between the stately progress of the buses and the taxis pulling up outside Claridge's.

Or, step out of Handel's long-vanished lodgings in Abbey Street, Dublin, head across the Liffey by the Ha'penny Bridge towards the grey towers of Christ Church Cathedral, and you are following in the composer's footsteps as he walked out one morning the following spring to reveal his *Messiah* to the world for the very first time.

Handel made his home in these busy new districts of the growing, prosperous, enlightened, gregarious capital cities of the kingdom. In 1736, thirteen years after he moved into what is now no. 25, the surveyor Robert Seymour described Brook Street in London as 'for the most part nobly built and inhabited by People of Quality',[1] noting that while four of its first inhabitants had been tradesmen, by 1736 seven of its forty-three rated

Copy after Thomas Hudson's magnificent portrait of Handel, c.1748 houses were occupied by titled residents. Similarly, Dublin, though much smaller than rapidly expanding London, was described by the mapmaker John Rocque in 1756 as 'one of the finest and largest Cities of Europe ... on Account of several spacious and magnificent Streets, the Gardens, Walks, &c.', whose inhabitants are 'frank, polite, affable, make it their Pleasure to live much with each other, and their Honour to treat Strangers with Politeness and Civility'.[2] These were Handel's neighbours, friends, customers, audience, collaborators, supporters and (occasionally) rivals.

As well as the physical and social contexts, *Messiah* was a child of its intellectual and philosophical context. Religion and politics clashed (as always) in the rival claims for the British throne, with very direct personal consequences for Handel's collaborator on *Messiah*, the librettist Charles Jennens. Philosophers and churchmen argued eloquently and passionately over their clerical bands and coffee cups and in the columns of publications like the *Spectator* about how religious observance should be organized. *Messiah* came at a point when the English Protestant experience of God was personal, inclusive, rational and faithful. John Locke's preface to *The Reasonableness of Christianity* states the case clearly: 'nothing is required to be believed by any Christian Man, but this, That Jesus is the Messiah.'[3] Deists sought to minimize the active engagement of the Creator in human affairs: *Messiah* was, in the words of one of its most insightful modern chroniclers, 'an assertion of everything that the Deists sought to deny'.[4]

This was an age rich in colourful characters, as this story will make abundantly clear – the talented, wayward and eccentric, the melancholic, the mad, the bad, the devout, the devoted and the downright dangerous. It was an age when bad behaviour was not necessarily a bar to social acceptance and considerable public success: some of the individuals in this story behaved very badly indeed. It's a story which takes in 'young men and maidens, old men and children',[5] as the psalmist says – choristers, orphans, theatrical impresarios, foreigners, jealous husbands with plenty

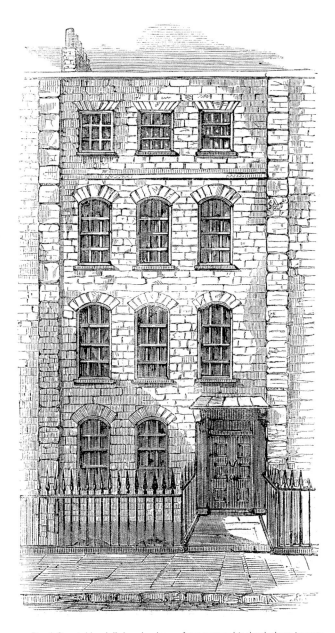

25 Brook Street, Handel's London home from 1723 to his death there in 1759.

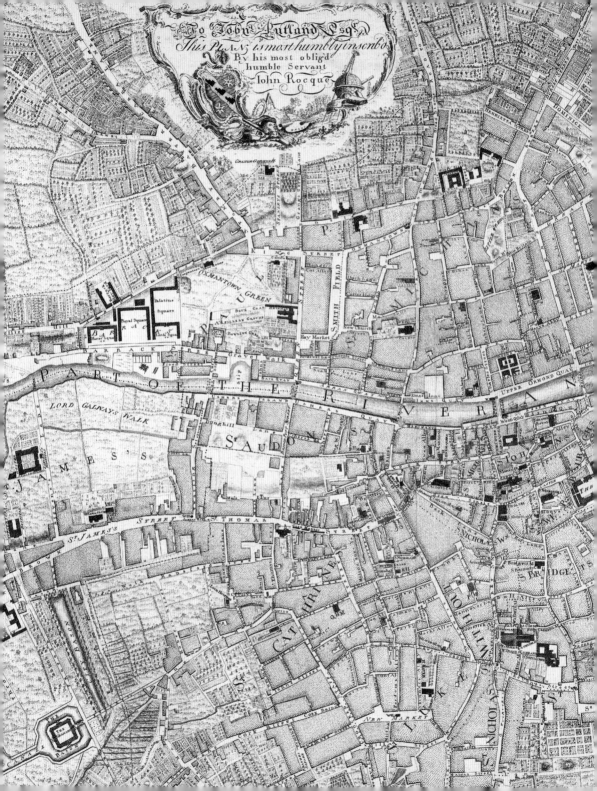

to be jealous about, divas, actresses, and a strong thread of the notable eighteenth-century tendency to charity and philanthropy.

And, for all its achievements in art and philosophy, this was an era which set great store by pleasure and having fun, and was perfectly willing to laugh at itself. In 1737, Henry Carey and composer John Frederick Lampe produced an English burlesque which mercilessly parodied the 'Nonsense, so prevailing in *Italian Operas*', and Handel in particular. It was called *The Dragon of Wantley*: the eponymous Dragon (sung by Henry Reinhold, one of Handel's favoured soloists, later a regular in his performances of *Messiah*) is defeated by the hero Moore of Moore-Hall. Gaffer Gubbins rewards Moore with the hand of his daughter Margery, and Gubbins and the chorus end the festivities by pointing the way to the musical future – not opera, but oratorio:

> *Gubbins:*
> Most mighty *Moore*, what Wonders hast thou done,
> Destroy'd the Dragon, and my *Margery* won,
> The Loves of this brave Knight, and my fair Daughter,
> In *Roratorios* shall be sung hereafter.
>
> *Chorus:*
> *Sing, sing, and rorio,*
> *An Oratorio*
> *To gallant* Morio ...[6]

This was the world into which *Messiah* was born.

Dublin as Handel knew it: John Rocque's map of 1757.

1

HANDEL'S WORLD
Germany, Italy, London, Dublin

George Frideric Handel was a remarkable character even by the standards of the great composers.

A whistle-stop tour through his earlier career reveals some of the influences and circumstances which led to *Messiah*.

As a child in provincial Halle in the last years of the seventeenth century, he benefitted from the attentions of a fine organist and teacher, Friedrich Wilhelm Zachow, who not only gave him a thorough grounding in the fugues and chorales which were the Lutheran musician's daily bread, but also introduced him to the work of a wide range of contemporary composers, much of it with an international accent. Gregarious and restless, at around the age of eighteen he met the Leipzig-based composer and law student Georg Philipp Telemann. This was the start of a fruitful friendship which was still going strong some half a century later when the two ageing composers corresponded about gardening, leading Handel to send Telemann a box of exotic plants as a gift. In 1703 Handel moved to Hamburg, where he composed his first operas. From 1706, now in his early twenties, he spent around three years in Italy, cultivating acquaintances with composers and cardinals, writing maybe a hundred secular vocal cantatas, taking his first

Vauxhall Pleasure Gardens (from Pyne's *Microcosm of London*, c.1809), where Handel's *Music for the Royal Fireworks* was first rehearsed.

steps into oratorio, and putting a firework under the Italian sacred choral style in a couple of effervescent psalm settings. All this shows up in *Messiah*.

In 1710 Handel became Kapellmeister (music director) to Prince George, Elector of Hanover, later George I of England. That same year he made a musically productive visit to London, and in 1712 decided to settle there.

Handel's contemporaries reveal the people around him through articles, reviews and, above all, letters. There is a certain amount of courtly formality about this mode of expression, but at the same time correspondents were more than ready to say what they thought of each other. Real affection is here: his neighbour and long-standing supporter Mary Delany referred to him as 'our friend Handel', commenting touchingly about a performance that seemed to have gone well: 'I love to have him pleased.'[1] The Earl of Shaftesbury called him 'the Old Buck'.[2] There was also plenty of room for rivalry and rudeness. Partisans coalesced into claques on each side, often using their musical preferences as a proxy for their own spats and divisions. The poet, hymn-writer and pioneer of a form of shorthand John Byrom compares Handel with the London-based Italian composer Giovanni Bononcini in some characteristically caustic versifying:

> Some say, compar'd to Bononcini,
> That Mynheer Handel's but a Ninny;
> Others aver, that he to Handel
> Is scarcely fit to hold a Candle:
> Strange all this Difference should be,
> 'Twixt Tweedle-dum and Tweedle-dee![3]

Unusually among the great composers of the seventeenth and eighteenth centuries, Handel was to some extent his own master. It is true that he actively sought, and found, gainful employment with royal and noble patrons, and that he took care to nurture and respect those working relationships. But at the same time, he enjoyed a far greater freedom from civic, ecclesiastical or aristocratic diktat than, for example, Bach or Telemann, or indeed Haydn or Mozart. His working relationship with the English monarchy is a good example. In 1713 he was granted a pension of £200 per annum, renewed by his old employer the Elector of Hanover when he became King George I in 1714. Minutes of the meeting of the directors of the Royal Academy of Music (an opera company financed by a joint stock venture and a royal bounty) of 30 November 1719 record 'And that Mr Hendell be Ma[ste]r of the Orchester with a Sallary' (though without further detail of amounts or length of payment: the Academy only managed to pay a dividend once, despite, or perhaps because of, some highly optimistic forecast returns).[4] In 1723 he was awarded a second additional pension and was made 'Composer of Musick for the Chapel Royal'. Other holders of that title, before and after, combined it with the day-to-day duties of chapel organist, writing small-scale service music as well as pieces for the big occasions. Not Handel.

A letter from Handel to Jennens, written at a significant moment in this story, makes the point well. Handel was in Ireland, and wished to extend his stay 'to have some more performances, when the 6 nights of the Subscription are over, and my Lord Duc the Lieutenant (who is allways present with all His Family on those Nights) will easily obtain a longer Permission for me by His Majesty ...'.[5] Two things stand out from this sentence: first, Handel recognized that he needed the King's permission to stay away a bit longer; second, he showed not the slightest doubt that he would get it. If Handel wanted to stay and make music in Ireland, then Handel stayed.

At least from the mid-1730s Handel became, in effect, a freelance composer. As his career and reputation developed, he increasingly took on the responsibility and risk for all aspects of his opera and oratorio seasons: booking the theatre or hall, finding the singers (often from abroad), selling tickets from the street frontage of his house in Brook Street, powdering his wig at showtime to stride through the streets and squares to Covent Garden or the Haymarket to conduct the performance from the keyboard, collecting the takings and paying the porters and performers. Generally speaking he was pretty good at it, though his finances could certainly become stretched at times if a particular piece fell foul of public taste or the spoiling tactics of a rival, leaving him temporarily unable to pay his expensive new signing from Italy. Sometimes a one-off benefit concert would restore financial equilibrium.

Much of the management was in the hands of his friend and amanuensis John Christopher Smith, like Handel an anglicized émigré from Germany. Smith was born Johann Christoph Schmidt in Ansbach, Bavaria. He came to England around 1716 expressly to act as Handel's financial assistant, and in due course took on the management of many aspects of his career. In later years parts of the role passed to his son, also John Christopher.

In between seasons Handel would compose new works. Operas and, later, oratorios were 'composed to be put "into the bank" for a ... season whose outlines and performers were as yet undefined',[6] as one eminent Handelian has it. When he did secure the services of his soloists, he would quite happily revisit his score and adjust keys and other details to suit the singers at hand. If a work proved popular, further changes would follow to accommodate a change of cast or venue for a revival the following season. It was a creative routine which Mozart, Verdi, Cole Porter and Irving Berlin would instantly have recognized and been entirely comfortable with. They were making great music, but they were also supplying a market, and they knew it.

The magnificently restored interior of Handel's home, 25 Brook Street, now the Handel House Museum. The portraits are of two of his musical colleagues, the celebrated soprano Faustina Bordoni, and bass singer Richard Leveridge.

JOHN CHRISTOPHER SMITH.

From an Original Picture Painted by Zoffani.

Published May 1.1799. by Cadell & Davies Strand

Handel's right-hand man, John Christopher Smith, who made the beautiful fair copy
of the score of *Messiah* which Handel used for all his performances.

Handel lived and moved and had his musical being at the centre of a gregarious network of friends, aficionados and fellow musicians. It was a tight-knit world, and very often musicians from one part of his musical life would reappear in another. At least one, possibly two, of the adult soloists at the first performances of *Messiah* in Dublin had sung for Handel as boys at the Chapel Royal in London. Opera soloists also sang for him in oratorios. Nor was this sociable cross-pollination limited to musicians: Dr Delany, the chancellor of St Patrick's Cathedral, Dublin at the time of the first *Messiah* performances, married Handel's friend and neighbour from Brook Street, Mary Pendarves. Another London neighbour, the 3rd Duke of Devonshire, crossed the Irish Sea the other way to become Lord Lieutenant of Ireland in 1733, where he played a key role in Handel's decision to try his chances there in late 1741.

There is a strong spirit of place, the *genius loci*, in Handel's output: the harpsichord suites he played to entertain a party at a friend's house, the intimate formality of his church music for the small Tudor spaces of the Chapel Royal or the grander canvas of Westminster Abbey, the *Water Music* wafting across the Thames. Perhaps in one of the sprightlier *Messiah* choruses we can hear him striding along the Strand or down Lower Ormond Quay, settling on the tempo he is going to take from the brisk rhythm of his own footsteps walking quickly, which in musical terms is *andante allegro*. These things reveal Handel quite as much as the many letters written to, about and (much less often) by the composer himself.

Few clues show through regarding his religious convictions. He signed off *Messiah* with *SDG*, for *Solo Deo Gloria*, or 'To God alone the Glory': he was a regular attender at the brand new parish church at the end of his street, St George's, Hanover Square. But this is conventional stuff. His sacred music reveals little: texts tend to be canticles, occasional pieces like coronation anthems, or the kind of verses earlier ages would have called 'indifferent' – middling in mood. His biblical oratorios focus unflinchingly on the human, not the divine. Unlike Bach, there is little theology in Handel. It's an aspect which has fed into the sometimes rather puzzled interpretation of *Messiah* over the centuries.

What has intrigued students of Handel even more is the complete lack of evidence of any romantic, emotional or sexual relationship of any kind. This doesn't mean they didn't happen, of course – George III, of all people, apparently reported that Handel had 'Amours ... of rather short duration, always within the pale of his own profession',[7] which is certainly credible – but there remains no evidence. Naturally, many theories have sprung up to fill the vacuum. Perhaps the truth is that he was one of those big personalities who don't need much emotional support. He certainly wasn't solitary – one of the great joys of musical life, then as now, is its immense sociability. Handel met a wide range of people socially and professionally and clearly enjoyed it. Perhaps, when the busy day was over, he preferred to end it in his own company rather than anyone else's, seeking 'rest unto his soul'. When composing, he needed the freedom to focus his time and energy into his work, safe from distractions and competing claims. It's a personality which recurs among creative types throughout the ages. Perhaps we should take the lack of evidence at face value, and not try to fill in the gaps with phantom lovers and anachronistic theories. We should let Handel be Handel.

Messiah is a work of full, reflective maturity. Its ebullient, irascible, larger-than-life composer was around fifty when oratorio began to seep into his opera seasons, adding spice and variety, and, later, taking over entirely. This medium matched his humanity and his experience perfectly.

Westminster Bridge, painted by Canaletto in 1747, shortly after it was built as the second river crossing in London.

2

THE SACRED ORATORIO
Form and context

'Handel has set up an Oratorio against the Operas, and succeeds,' wrote that witty and waspish observer of eighteenth-century life, Horace Walpole, in February 1742/3. 'He has hired all the goddesses from farces and the singers of *Roast Beef* from between the acts at both theatres, with a man with one note in his voice, and a girl without ever an one; and so they sing, and make brave hallelujahs; and the good company encore the recitative, if it happens to have an cadence like what they call a tune.'[1]

Walpole was writing less than a year after the advent of *Messiah*. A couple of years earlier James Grassineau's *Musical Dictionary* had defined the new beast:

> ORATORIO, a sort of spiritual opera full of dialogues, recitatives, duettos, trios, ritornellos, choruses &c., the subject thereof is usually taken from the scripture, or is the life and actions of some saint, &c. The music for the *Oratorio* should be in the finest state, and most chosen strains. The words hereof are often in *Latin*, sometimes in *French* and *Italian*, and among us even in *English*. These *Oratorios* are greatly used at *Rome* in time of *Lent*; here indeed they are used in no other season.[2]

Chorus of Singers, an etching of an apparently rather ramshackle chorus, by William Hogarth, 1732.

Also in 1740 the *Bibliothèque Britannique* observed that 'l'ORATORIO est une espece d'Opéra qu'on pourroit définir *l'Opéra Sacré* ou *l'Opéra Spirituel* ...', tracing its origins in Rome, and tellingly noting the avoidance of 'la pompe ordinaire du Théâtre' and strict observance of 'certains Réglemens touchant les Spectacles ... l'*Oratorio* n'admet ni Habillemens de Théâtre, ni Machines, ni changemens de Décorations, ni Danses, ni allées & venues de la part des ... Acteurs, ou Musiciens chantans ...'[3] Such 'réglemens' were a key factor in the development of oratorio up to this point.

These detailed descriptions not only give the background to the Handelian oratorio, but also show how far he moved beyond his inheritance: far from being simply 'the life and actions of some saint', his mature works in the form are cosmic psychodramas of the human condition, as profound and insightful as any work of musical drama, of any age, anywhere.

The Roman connection links the word to the chapels (or 'oratories', in English) of the followers of St Philip Neri, where narrative episodes of liturgy and Scripture were performed to specially composed music. Dramatic treatment of sacred subjects was not confined to Catholic countries, of course: the medieval English tradition of mystery plays fed into the fashionable Elizabethan fad for secular choirboy theatricals, most notably those performed by the Chapel Royal company, a tradition which petered out under pressure of Puritanism, politics and poor management about a century before Handel took up his duties there. Something of the dramatic approach to the sacred survived in the solo *scenas* of later seventeenth-century composers like John Blow and Henry Purcell, whose *In guilty night (Saul and the Witch of Endor)* chillingly prefigures Handel's own setting of the same scene in his gory masterpiece *Saul*. The verse anthem alternates solo voices with passages for choir: an example like Pelham Humfrey's apocalyptic 'Hear, O heavens' almost turns choral singers into stage characters by using texts with a first-person narrator ('I have nourished and brought up children, and they have rebelled against me'; 'Ah! Sinful nation!').

Georgio II.^{do} *Mag: Brit: Franc: & Hiber: Regi*

Nuptias Ceremoniales inter Annam Mag: Brit: Principissam Regalem et Gulielmum Principem
Araussionensem habitas in Capella Regia S.^{ti} Jacobi apud Londinum Martis 14^{ti}: An:1733.
Devotissimus et obligatissimus servus Gul: Kent.
Humillime offert, dicat, dedicatque

The Queen's Chapel, now part of the Chapel Royal establishment at St James's Palace, on the occasion of the wedding of Anne, Princess Royal to the Prince of Orange, 14 March 1733/4. The princess was a keen Handelian, and Handel composed the fine anthem 'This is the Day' for the occasion.

Purcell's symphony anthems go one stage further by adding overtures and interludes for a small orchestra, often in dance-type forms, carrying more than a whiff of the greasepaint and footlights into church (to the dismay of some of their early listeners).[4] Odes to St Cecilia developed the idea of a sung narrative, religious but not liturgical, dramatic but not theatrical.

Handel took all this and made of it something new and entirely his own. As the scholar Jens Peter Larsen put it, 'Handelian oratorio is not simply a stage in the general development of oratorio but to a great extent a unique art-form.'[5] That art-form developed and expanded with each work. *Messiah* is simply the most unusual and original in a body of works, each of which is unique in its own way.

Its antecedents in Handel's working life show that development in progress. As a young man, Handel was well versed in the tradition of German Passion settings, and composed one himself in about 1716. The form has clear links into Part Two of *Messiah*, where the alternation of sung narrative and choral comment is subtly transformed into something more fluid and universal. In Italy he composed two oratorios, *Il Trionfo del Tempo e del Disinganno* and, for Easter Sunday 1708, *La Resurrezione*. Again, the pre-echoes of *Messiah* sound loud and clear.

Esther, generally thought of as Handel's first English oratorio, has an interesting genesis. It began life as a masque called simply 'Oratorium' for Cannons, the rococo Middlesex mansion of Handel's patron James Brydges, Earl of Carnarvon, around 1718–20. Much later, in spring 1731/2, the Chapel Royal choirmaster Bernard Gates performed it in a revised and expanded version with his Chapel singers at the Crown and Anchor tavern in the Strand (and possibly also in his own house in James Street). These were private performances, staged and in costume. Handel was sufficiently encouraged by the favourable reception to add the work to his season at the King's Theatre that May, partly because Princess Anne wanted to hear it,[6] and presented a revised and expanded version in concert form, with singers

A notice of the 1732 performance of the oratorio *Esther*, a significant step
in Handel's constant evolution of the form.

drawn from the opera, but with no scenery or action. The English oratorio
was born, almost by accident.

Several points emerge from this process. First, the iterative nature
of Handel's compositional method: there are different versions, with
different titles, as the work morphed and modulated to suit each season's
circumstances and soloists. This was accompanied by the usual caustic
comments from the more partisan elements of public and press: 'Senesino
and *Bertolli* made rare work with the *English* Tongue you would have sworn
it had been *Welch*,'[7] said one; another reported that one of the soloists made
the line 'I come, my queen, to chaste delights' sound like 'I comb my queen to
chase the lice'.[8] Second, part of that iterative process was the incorporation
of music taken from other pieces, in this case the 1727 coronation anthems.
Third, the close working relationship with a clearly highly accomplished

group of Chapel Royal singers – one of the treble soloists in the 1732 *Esther* was John Beard, later one of Handel's regular tenor soloists in *Messiah*, and Gates went on to supply several more generations of well-trained trebles for the *Messiah* chorus. Fourth, and perhaps most important of all, the prospect of choristers appearing on stage did not go down terribly well with the clerical authorities: Burney reported that 'the Princess Royal ... was pleased to express a desire to see it [*Esther*] exhibited in action at the Opera-house in the Hay-market, by the same young performers; but Dr. Gibson, then Bishop of London, would not grant permission for its being represented on that stage, even with books in the children's hands.'[9] Edmund Gibson was also dean of the Chapel Royal – he was probably as much concerned about the standard of the boys' daily musical duties there as he was about their moral welfare. The resourceful Handel, as usual, found a way round the problem: 'Mr. HANDEL, however, the next year, had it performed at that theatre, with additions to the Drama, by Humphreys; but in *still life*; that is, without action, in the same manner as Oratorios have been since constantly performed.'[10] A newspaper advertisement made it clear that 'There will be no Action on the Stage, but the House will be fitted up in a decent Manner for the Audience, the Musick to be disposed after the Manner of the Coronation Service.'[11]

It all speaks to the ambiguous status of oratorio. In one respect, oratorio only existed at all because opera stopped in Lent, and a succession of deans and bishops feared that composers and promoters simply transferred their musical and dramatic fancy to Holy Writ in order to carry on feeding the public appetite. In many ways they were absolutely right.

The 1730s was the key decade for the advance of oratorio. In 1733 Handel was invited to Oxford, where he gave his enthusiastic audience 'a spick and span new Oratorio called *Athalia*',[12] along with *Deborah* and *Esther*. In 1735 he began adding concertos between the acts of his oratorios. Later in the decade he commissioned a new organ which he could see over while

The first theatre in the Haymarket, which burned down in 1789.
Watercolour by William Capon (1757–1827).

playing, 'so constructed that as he sits at it he has a better command of his performers than he used to have, and he is highly delighted to think with what exactness his Oratorio will be performed by the help of this Organ; so that for the future instead of beating time at his oratorios, he is to sit at the Organ all the time with his back to the Audience',[13] as Jennens reported to a cousin. *Alexander's Feast* of 1736 is a sort of hybrid, an ode about the power of music.

In 1737, a revised London version of the Roman oratorio *Il Trionfo*, sung in Italian, was performed four times. In April of the same year, however, Handel suffered a stroke. Though recovery was rapid and remarkably complete, progress towards the new art-form inevitably slowed.

The next big step came the following year. Its origins lay in some correspondence between Handel and Jennens three years earlier, in the summer of 1735. Handel wrote:

> I received your very agreeable Letter with the inclosed Oratorio. I am just going to Tunbridge, yet what I could read of it in haste, gave me a great deal of Satisfaction. I shall have more leisure time there to read it with all the Attention it deserves. There is no certainty of any Scheme for next Season, but it is probable that some thing or other may be done, of which I shall take the Liberty to give you notice, being extreamly obliged to you for the generous Concern you show upon this account.[14]

The 'inclosed' was *Saul*. Composed three years later, in 1738, *Saul* set the style and standard for Handel's mature biblical oratorios, and it remains one of the great works of musical drama.

The splendid 1756 portrait of Handel by Thomas Hudson, who gives no indication that the composer was by now quite blind. This is known as the Gopsall portrait, after the country house built by Charles Jennens, librettist of *Messiah*, who commissioned it.

The year 1739 saw another entirely original conception, *Israel in Egypt*. Here, Handel gave Scripture's pictures of frogs, boils, locusts, flies and various other plagues almost entirely to the chorus, and, significantly, used the text as it is in the Bible, not rendered into verse. This, naturally, unleashed another salvo in the ongoing skirmish about the propriety of singing sacred words in the theatre. Some took Handel's side, berating the 'stupid, senseless *Exceptions* that have been taken to so truly Religious Representations, as *this*, in particular, and the other *Oratorios* are, from the *Place* they are *exhibited* in'.[15]

Opera increasingly occupied less of Handel's musical horizons. The winter season of 1740/1 saw just two stage works from Handel's pen, *Imeneo* and *Deidamia*, which ran for two and three performances respectively to February 1740/1. They were to be Handel's last operas.

On 10 July 1741 Jennens wrote to his friend Edward Holdsworth:

> Handel says he will do nothing next Winter, but I hope I shall perswade him to set another Scripture Collection I have made for him, & perform it for his own Benefit in Passion Week. I hope he will lay out his whole genius & Skill upon it, that the Composition may excell all his former Compositions, as the Subject excells every other Subject. The Subject is Messiah.[16]

The phrase 'another Scripture Collection' has been taken by scholars to imply that Jennens had also assembled the text of the earlier *Israel in Egypt*. This seems entirely plausible, though there is no direct evidence. In any event, the auguries for the new venture were good: composer and librettist had an established working relationship, each equally demanding of the other; Jennens knew from practical experience how to turn his deep knowledge of the Bible into a well-shaped libretto; Handel responded with an ever more inventive and highly personal synthesis of ode, anthem, opera and aria, with, crucially, the chorus taking centre stage.

The stars were aligned.

A 3ᵈ Set of

HANDEL'S SONGS

Selected from His Latest ORATORIOS

For the

HARPSICORD, VOICE, HOBOY or GERMAN FLUTE.

The Instrumental Parts to the above Songs may be had Seperate to Compleat them for Concerts.

London. *Printed for* I. Walsh, *in Catharine Street, in the Strand.*

Of whom may be had, Compos'd by Mr Handel.

Oratorios.			
Judas Macchabeus	Deborah	L'Allegro il Penserofo	Apollo's Feaft, 500 Songs from the late Operas.
Belthazzar	Hercules	Athalia	The Coronation and Funeral Anthem, and Te Deum.
Occafional Oratorio	Semele	Efther	Twelve Solos for a German Flute and Harpficord.
Jofeph	Alexander's Feaft	Saul	Sonatas, or Chamber Aires from all the Operas and
Samfon	Acis and Galatea	Dryden's Ode on St Cecilia	Oratorios, Set for a German Flute and a Bafs.
			Two Sets of Leffons, 54 Overtures, and 12 Concertos
			for the Harpficord.

The title page of a collection of individual numbers extracted from Handel's oratorios, arranged by John Walsh and published in 1749.

3

CHARLES JENNENS, LIBRETTIST

The other maker of *Messiah* reveals a different side of eighteenth-century intellectual life.

Charles Jennens (pronounced and often written at the time as 'Jennings') was fifteen years younger than Handel, a patron of the arts, generous philanthropist and wealthy landowner 'born and bred in Leicestershire mud',[1] as he put it. He lost several members of his family in his youth and early adulthood, including a gifted younger brother to a particularly gruesome suicide, apparently as a result of a religious crisis. Enlightenment questioning of the old certainties had its downsides. Perhaps unsurprisingly in the light of this troubled start in life, Jennens remained unmarried and often solitary, prone to 'Perturbations and Anxieties of the Mind, and not infrequently an extreme Lowness and Depression of Spirits',[2] in the words of the perceptive oration at his funeral in 1773.

Jennens was a non-juror. Non-jurors refused to swear allegiance to the Hanoverian dynasty because they did not recognize the execution of Charles I or the overthrow of James II as legitimate. As a result, official preferment and employment were, to a large extent, denied him. Like many non-jurors, he was simultaneously a passionate high church Anglican, who

Charles Jennens, *Messiah*'s librettist. Another rich portrait by Hudson, one of two of Jennens, probably dating from the mid-1740s, shortly after the first performances of *Messiah*.

found himself paradoxically supporting the claims of a Catholic King. This troublesome contradiction is perhaps best illustrated by imagining Jennens leading prayers in the elegant chapel at the magnificent country house which he built at Gopsall in Leicestershire, standing in front of an altar made from an oak tree which had sheltered the future Charles II after the battle of Worcester, reading to his household from the Book of Common Prayer and omitting all mention of the legally anointed King of England.

He was a scholar and a divine, with a deep knowledge of his Bible and ready to raid it for political messaging in his librettos and other writings. He was a pioneering editor of Shakespeare, producing a remarkably modern edition in which he sought to collate different readings in search of an authoritative text, rather different to the approach of older contemporaries like Nahum Tate, who would quite happily add both a rape scene and a happy ending to *King Lear* because that's what their audience wanted.

He was a melancholic, capable of profound generosity and catty criticism, both of which add spice to his ample output of letters. His principal correspondent was his friend Edward Holdsworth, who emerges as something of a hero in this story: a wise counsellor, always ready to talk him down from the extremes of mood swing and impolitic opinion in his letters, and a supplier of music from his travels (which he bought by weight 'because as you know I am perfectly ignorant of music')[3] to help soothe his troubled soul, as it did for the mighty Saul, one of the most vivid and recognizably fallible human characters in Jennens' libretti for Handel, a figure drawn from his knowledge and experience of tragedy, Shakespearean and his own. Jennens owned one of the very first pianos in England, which Handel played.

His collaboration with Handel showed the characteristic combination of successful symbiosis and bickering disagreement with which composers and wordsmiths have fertilized their working relationships in every musical age. They were quite ready to criticize and question each other's choices and judgements, but they remained on good terms through their fairly brief but intensely productive period of collaboration and beyond. It's probably right to infer that their creative tensions improved the quality of their work.

Jennens and Handel worked together closely in the period leading up to *Messiah*. The libretto for *Saul* is divided into 'numbers', as were most oratorios of the time, full of subtle metrical and rhythmic variety and drawing on a huge range of source and reference. Handel treated this schema with considerable freedom. For example, in the epic lament for the golden youth Jonathan, he shifts from chorus to solo in the middle of a rhyming couplet:

> *Chorus:* O fatal Day! How low the Mighty lie!
> *David:* O Jonathan! How nobly didst thou die,

This allows David to speak the name of his lost friend, on his own: corporate condolence moves to private grief. The music lets us feel the knife twisting in David's heart. Throughout, Handel manipulated forces and form to focus unsparingly on moments of intense personal crisis: Saul's jealousy and despair; the Witch (a tenor) in a diabolical mixture of 3/4 and 4/4 time, summoning Samuel spookily from the grave to the sepulchral sound of bassoons; David's heartbreaking elegy for Jonathan. In Handel's hands the chorus is bloody, bold and resolute. The orchestration generally is rich and varied, including harp and trombones.

Sometimes, fascinatingly, Jennens called the musical shots. When David gets the news that the Amalekite has killed the wounded Saul, he spits the first words of his furious aria, 'Impious wretch', at the hapless messenger before the *ritornello* to the aria begins. This is not how aria form usually works, and close examination of the handwriting in the manuscript shows that it was Jennens' idea. It works brilliantly: the singer playing David can react with instant rage and a top D ringing with indignation. Similarly,

Saul's death is reported to David in the autograph of Handel's oratorio *Saul*, words by Jennens, composed in 1738. Jennens has added the first two words and three notes to Handel's score.

Handel tried to graft a gratuitous 'Hallelujah' chorus onto the end, where, according to Jennens, it 'comes in very nonsensically, having no manner of relation to what goes before'.[4] Jennens was right: and he won (the chorus was relocated to Part One).

David's aria from Part III of *Saul*, the moment when the Amalekite confesses he has just killed Saul.

More relevantly to the first audiences, the story of Saul formed part of the annual commemoration of the execution of Charles I. Jennens' biographer Ruth Smith comments, 'In the vast amount of British debate about the lawfulness of the changes of rulership from Stuarts to Hanoverians, both sides constantly evoked the story of Saul and David. ... For Jennens ... the death of Saul had special, complicated resonance.'[5] 'By Thee the Lord's anointed died,' snarls David, eyeballing the Hanoverian establishment lined up in the front row in their hoops and ruffs.

Jennens slightly despaired of some of Handel's more extravagant plans:

Mr. Handel's head is more full of Maggots than ever: I found yesterday in His room a very queer Instrument which He calls Carillon (Anglice a Bell) ... & with this Cyclopean Instrument he designs to make poor Saul stark mad ... I could tell you more of his Maggots: but it grows late, and I must defer the rest till I write next; by which time, I doubt not, more new ones will breed in his Brain ...[6]

A year on from *Saul*, Jennens was probably responsible for the text of *Israel in Egypt*, a Biblical anthology like *Messiah*. About a year after that, in 1739/40, Jennens supplied Handel with a third poem to go with Milton's odes to the humours, *L'Allegro* and *Il Penseroso*, which he called *Il Moderato* (perhaps not a bad analogy for Holdsworth's attempts to reconcile the two poles of his own personality). Rather later, in 1744, came *Belshazzar,* which in some respects links the promised return of God's people to their homeland to the expected restoration of the Stuart Kings of England even more explicitly than *Saul*.

Handel's late oratorios are wonderful pieces. His best librettists shared his instinct for focusing in on the lives, loves and losses of the protagonists, moving fluently from the universal to the personal. Fate marches towards a moment of crisis and bitter self-awareness: Saul seeking counsel from Hell; Jephtha trading victory for the life of his own daughter. These are among the great moments of music as drama.

They also show just how unusual and original a conception *Messiah* is.

Anthologizing a sacred text at this time was a Protestant notion. Gibbons and Purcell both set psalm texts but felt entirely free to leave half-verses out because it suited the music. The coronation text 'My heart is inditing' is a collage of varied verses crafted by a priestly librettist for Purcell in 1685: Handel filleted it further by setting only some of Purcell's text for George II's coronation of 1727. Later luminaries of English church music like S.S. Wesley became expert at gathering a text like a shepherd from all over their Bible by a kind of personalized concordance, linking themes, words and ideas across texts and testaments.

Messiah is the ultimate example of this process.

For example, the disjunct verses from Isaiah which prefigure the birth of the Saviour in the middle of Part One make many references to light which spark off each other. This image is then carried over and picked up in the Christmas scene when the glory of the Lord shines round about the fluttering angels. The Passion narrative is rendered with extraordinary subtlety in Part Two, not least because it contains almost nothing from the actual Gospel story, focusing instead on Psalms and Lamentations. Christ himself is only mentioned for the first time at the very end of Part Two. The theology, and the drama, are elusive, fluid and implicit. This is not a work which tells you what to think: instead, it invites you to listen, and think for yourself.

Jennens added two quotations to the title page of the text of *Messiah* for Handel's London performances in 1743. One is from Virgil: *Majora canamus* – 'We sing of higher things'. This indicates not only Jennens' considerable erudition, but also his wish to call on the wisdom of the ancients, whom he called the 'Heathen Poets', to be his witness. Like the text itself, his outlook encompasses the entire history of enlightened and educated human thought. The other superscription is from Paul's epistles to Timothy (3:16) and the Colossians (2:3):

And without controversy, great is the Mystery of Godliness: God was manifested in the Flesh, justify'd by the Spirit, seen of Angels, preached among the Gentiles, believed on in the World, received up in glory.

In whom are hid all the Treasures of Wisdom and Knowledge

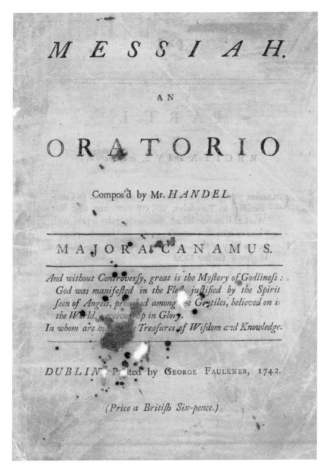

M E S S I A H.

A N

O R A T O R I O

Compos'd by Mr. *H A N D E L.*

M A J O R A *C A N A M U S.*

And without Controversy, great is the Mystery of Godliness :
God was manifested in the Flesh, justified by the Spirit
seen of Angels, preached among the Gentiles, believed on in
the World, received up in Glory.
In whom are hid all the Treasures of Wisdom and Knowledge.

DUBLIN Printed by GEORGE FAULKNER, 1742.

(Price a British Six-pence.)

A slightly decayed title page of an early word-book of *Messiah* for one of the first
performances in 1742, with the mottoes from Virgil and Scripture.

Here is *Messiah* in miniature, a compact of Jennens' complex and sometimes contradictory relationship with the religious temper of his times.

In 1743, in the printed word-books issued for the first London performances, Jennens subdivided his text into 'scenes', with some variation in
the exact wording between editions. Part One, for example, is presented as
five 'scenes':

(i) The prophecy of Salvation; (ii) the prophecy of the coming of Messiah and the question, despite (i), of what this may portend for the World; (iii) the prophecy of the Virgin Birth; (iv) the appearance of the Angels to the Shepherds; (v) Christ's redemptive miracles on earth.

The headings shine a light on how Jennens linked his texts together. For example, in Part Two Isaiah's 'How beautiful are the feet' and St Paul's 'Their sound is gone out' are followed by the psalmist's 'Why do the nations so furiously rage together'. The link can sound a bit bumpy: like the psalmist, we wonder exactly why the nations are raging at this point. Jennens' headings explain that 'scene' VI represents 'Whitsun, and the subsequent preaching of the Gospel', which leads straight into 'scene' VII, 'The world's hostile reception to the Gospel'. The raging makes sense.

The textual scheme also reveals how much Jennens decided not to say: in Part Two, 'scene' II, Christ's death and resurrection are treated briefly, almost perfunctorily, without mentioning Christ. What happened is not really important; or, at least, is taken as read. What matters is why it happened, and what it means to us, the listeners.

There are many subtle changes in the words between the sources in Scripture and the finished libretto. Often, these alter first person to third. For example, St Matthew's 'come unto me, all ye that labour' becomes 'come unto him' to match the paired verses from Isaiah, 'He shall feed his flock'. Another aria changes both person and tense to achieve consistency: 'He is despised' becomes 'He was despised', and 'I gave my back to the smiters' is rendered as 'He gave his back'. It is all immensely fluid and subtle, testament to Jennens' care, skill and ability to make connections across his Bible.

At least one significant change to the words appears to have been Handel's doing, since it was made in Dublin when Jennens wasn't there: Handel chose to set St Paul's version of 'How beautiful are the feet', rather than the original verses from Isaiah which St Paul is quoting. It's a little difficult to unpick the significance of this – in any event, Jennens allowed it to stand (or failed to 'perswade' Handel to change it).

Perhaps unsurprisingly with these two, their working relationship on *Messiah* was not entirely straightforward. If anything, Handel comes across as the more emollient. He took care to give Jennens his share of the credit for the success of the first performances, neatly referring to 'your oratorio Messiah' in his letters home from Dublin:

> Your humble servant ... intended you a visit in my way from Ireland to London, for I certainly could have given you a better account by word of mouth, as by writing, how well your Messiah was received in that Country ...[7]

Jennens could, as usual, simultaneously adore Handel's music to the point of idolatry, and feel that the composer wasn't trying hard enough:

> He has made a fine Entertainment of it, tho' not near so good as he might & ought to have done. I have with great difficulty made him correct some of the grossest faults in the composition, but he retain'd his Overture obstinately, in which there are some passages far unworthy of Handel, but much more unworthy of the Messiah ...[8]

adding elsewhere

> As to the Messiah, 'tis still in his power by retouching the weak parts to make it fit for a public performance; & I have said a great deal to him on the Subject: but he is so lazy & so obstinate, that I much doubt the effect.[9]

He was also quite capable of taking Handel's supposed deficiencies as a personal slight:

A relatively small number of letters by Handel survive, a mixture of business and personal matters, in English, French and German. Here, on 19 July 1744, he writes to Jennens about *Belshazzar*, their collaboration after *Messiah*, and tactfully asks Jennens to 'point out these passages in the Messiah which you think require altering'.

> His Messiah has disappointed me; being set in great haste, tho' he said he would be a year about it, & make it the best of all his Compositions. I shall put no more sacred words into his hands, to be thus abus'd.[10]

This is at best a partial reading, deliberate or otherwise, of Handel's method: he did on occasion take up to a year to 'make' a work, but often worked fast, and certainly with no lack of quality.

Jennens apparently suggested some changes, which Handel was at pains to acknowledge: 'Be pleased to point out these passages in the Messiah which you think require altering.'[11] Jennens thought he knew why this was:

Handel has promis'd to revise the Oratorio of Messiah, & He and I are very good Friends again. The reason is, he has lately lost his Poet Miller, & wants to set me at work for him again. Religion & Morality, Gratitude, Good Nature and Good Sense had been better Principles of Action than this Single Point of Interest but I must take him as I find him and make the best use I can of him ...[12]

There is probably a touch of *amour-propre* here: Jennens was a better poet than the late Miller, and knew it.

Jennens even attempted to rewrite some of the music in *Messiah* (as indeed he did with other works by Handel), partly in a probably well-intentioned attempt to sort out some of Handel's dodgy English word underlay, partly to put the theological as well as the verbal stress where he felt it should go:

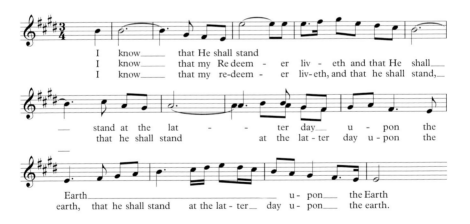

Versions and variants. Three different ways of fitting the words to a passage from the aria 'I know that my redeemer liveth'. The first line of lyrics shows Handel's first attempt, crossed out by him in the autograph. Below is his second (and final) go – he made many such changes in this piece. Third comes Jennens' effort, which even requires a rewrite of the music in one bar (stems down). These manuscript alterations are found in vol. 3 of the score formerly in the possession of the musicologist Sir Newman Flower, dated by Watkins Shaw as corresponding to the 1749 performance.[13] Larsen ascribes the handwriting to Jennens.[14]

Who is the King of Glory?
The Lord ftrong and mighty, the Lord mighty in
Battle.
Lift up your Heads O ye Gates, and be ye lift up ye
everlafting Doors, and the King of Glory fhall come in.
Who is the King of Glory?
The Lord of Hofts: He is the King of Glory.

RECITATIVE.

Unto which of the Angels faid he at any Time, Thou
art my Son, this Day have I begotten thee?

CHORUS.

Let all the Angels of God worfhip him.

AIR.

Thou art gone up on high, thou haft led Captivity captive, and received Gifts for Men, yea for thine Enemies,
that the Lord God might dwell among them.

CHORUS.

The Lord gave the Word; great was the Company
of the Preachers.

DUETTO and CHORUS.

How beautiful are the Feet of him that bringeth glad
Tidings, Tidings of Salvation! That faith unto *Zion*
thy God reigneth! Break forth into Joy, thy God
reigneth.

B   AIR.

A page from the word-book for the first Oxford performance of *Messiah* in 1749.

Jennens' view of the world, human and divine, was complex but of a piece. When Holdsworth died in 1746 Jennens raised a monument to him at Gopsall bearing the inscription 'Thanks be to God who gives us the Victory through our Lord Jesus Christ'.

Jennens was a loyal though critical friend, a deep, sad and wise thinker, and a fine writer. All this is in *Messiah*.

Handel's *Messiah* is Jennens' *Messiah*, too.

Allegro senza rip:

rejoyce rejoyce rejoyce — greatly

pian

pian

4

THE COMPOSITION OF *MESSIAH* AND HANDEL'S 'BORROWINGS'

Handel wrote *Messiah* miraculously quickly. He dated the various stages of the process precisely on his manuscript (using, rather oddly, astrological symbols for the days of the week): 'angefangen' [begun] Saturday 22 August 1741; Part One completed Friday 28 August; Part Two Sunday 6 September; Part Three Saturday 12 September; 'ausgefüllet' (literally 'filled up') 'den 14 dieses' ('the 14th this'). These gnomic polyglottisms tell us that he composed the three Parts in six, nine and six days respectively, then took just two days more to 'fill up' the orchestral detail, harmonies, doublings, word underlay and inner parts, finishing on 'the 14th of this [month]', September 1741.

It's an astonishing achievement, a creative genius engaging in bursts of activity which must then be matched with periods of stasis: Jennens described a type when he said 'Mr Handel has his fits of hard labour as well as of idleness.'[1]

Handel's manuscript shows the speed of work: blots, smudges, shorthand, verbal cues, crossings-out and show-throughs, note-tails and rests cut off. But clarity and precision of thought shine through – there are few slips, and his intentions are clear, even where he has changed his mind in the act of writing. It's a thrilling, living document, active and alive as Beethoven's manuscripts are, like something written by lightning.

A detail of Handel's annotations on the conducting score (see page 64).

Alongside the autograph, the other principal source of *Messiah* is the fair copy made by John Christopher Smith. This was Handel's conducting score for the rest of his life, constantly updated and annotated with the names of soloists and changes of version and key, and is thus a priceless record of the evolution of the work at the composer's own hands. Smith managed the copying of Handel's voluminous output alongside his other administrative and managerial roles for the composer. Much of it he did himself, the rest he delegated to an efficient team of subcontractors (anonymous scribes later forensically filleted out from each other by patient modern scholars from their handwriting, watermarks and other minutiae, silent witnesses providing precious clues to the hierarchy of sources).

There are a few surviving sketches, including the 'Amen', 'He was despised' and a theme which the composer seems to have tried out for both 'Let all the Angels' and 'Let us break their bonds'. There may well have been others, now lost.

More significant is Handel's habit of borrowing.

Building bits of other men's music into your own was an established part of compositional practice. At the same time, baroque music relied on a library of musical gestures (or 'affects') which the listener would know and recognize: lilting 6/8 melodies like a shepherd's song for a pastoral scene; fanfare-like triadic figures for a martial aria. These are not borrowings, they are references to a common repertoire of mood and manner. *Messiah* contains examples, like the charming pastoral 'Pifa' (see opposite).

In terms of reusing music from other sources, Handel borrowed more than most. It's a puzzling aspect of his genius, and proved occasionally contentious from the outset. Jennens owned a large library of music, and told Holdsworth in 1742/3 'Handel has borrow'd a dozen of the pieces, & I dare say I shall catch him stealing from them, as I have formerly'.[2] 'Stealing' is a strong word – all commentators acknowledge that Handel made more of other men's music than they did themselves. Perhaps this letter finds

Handel's composition autograph: the 'Pifa', the short orchestral interlude which introduces the scene with the shepherds by echoing the traditional tunes of the *pifferari,* Italian shepherds with their pipes. Many baroque compositions made this reference.

Jennens in one of his cattier moods. But it remains something of a puzzle why such a fluent genius needed the stimulus of other people's ideas. It's as if finding the initial spark was the hard part. Once he had it, he was off.

Messiah shows comparatively little borrowing by Handel's standards. Even more unusually, all the borrowing (at least, all the direct borrowing) is from his own works, and from just one category of works: secular Italian vocal duets. (By contrast, some 40 per cent of the music in *Israel in Egypt* derives from other composers, even more from his own earlier works, much of it via another piece, the extraordinary funeral anthem *The Ways of Zion do Mourn*, which he transplanted whole into the oratorio as Part One by changing the words). It is just one more example of how each work represents a unique approach to source, form and content.

Five movements in *Messiah* are based on his own Italian duets: 'And he shall purify', 'For unto us a child is born', 'His yoke is easy', 'All we like sheep', and 'O death, where is thy sting?' The sources are 'Quel fior che all'alba ride' (HWV 192, July 1741); 'No, di voi non vo' fidarmi (HWV 189, July 1741) and 'Se tu non lasci amore' (HWV 193, 1722). It was not the only time he raided a secular love song for holy things, just as a Renaissance composer like Lassus would happily have done. Of these five movements, the first four derive from duets composed just a few months before *Messiah*, as if the music was swirling around in his mind, ready to be turned to account as required. The last of the five stands slightly separate – it is based on a duet written some thirty years earlier, during his travels in Italy; it stayed as a duet in *Messiah* (though for different voices) while all the others were recast as four-part choruses; it is based much less closely on its original.

It can be slightly disorientating listening to these Italian duets and hearing such familiar music sung by different voices with different words in a different language – and especially to reflect that the Italian version came first. But the skill of the transformative process is clear: both versions are complete works of art in their own right. Part of the key to understanding Handel's constant borrowing can be found in just how good he was at it.

The attentive listener can catch occasional hints and pre-echoes of *Messiah* in other Handel works – the brief snatch of duet writing at 'To thee, Cherubim and Seraphim' from the 1713 Utrecht *Te Deum*; and 'Since by man ... / By man came also ...' in 'Their bodies are buried ... / But their name liveth ...' from the *The Ways of Zion do Mourn* of 1737 (music which the Handel scholar Donald Burrows has in turn traced to a model by the

The opening of the vocal duet 'Se tu non lasci amore', the musical model for 'O death, where is thy sting?' in *Messiah*. The second musical idea in the original duet is quite different in character from the second musical idea in the chorus. The cheery realization of the right-hand keyboard part used here (and later) is by Brahms, no less: like Mozart, he can't quite resist the temptation to include the occasional harmony not strictly indicated by Handel's figured bass in the original.

sixteenth-century composer Jakob Handl).[3] Another eminent Handelian, Jonathan Keates, has suggested a proto-source for the 'Amen' in an opera by Giovanni Porta.[4] Some musical ideas are generic: versions of the fugue subject at 'And with his stripes' turn up in Bach and Mozart, among others, but there's no suggestion of anyone borrowing from anyone else — it's just a good fugue subject.

Many investigators have looked for Lutheran chorales in Handel's sacred

Two more proto-sources. Comparison of these duet movements with their offspring in *Messiah* reveals Handel at work: the light two-part counterpoint translates into the choruses ('For unto us ...', 'and the government ...') while the four-part homophonic passages ('Wonderful, Counsellor ...', 'that they may offer unto the Lord ...') are newly composed; some of the melodies work better in *Messiah* than in their secular incarnation (the rising sequence at 'cieco amor' matches Isaiah's repetition of 'unto us' rather neatly); tunes reappearing in different keys in the duets become the fugal entries of the various voice parts in the choruses. Alongside the obvious self-borrowings, there is a certain similarity between 'Sò per prova' and the opening of 'Hallelujah!' (see in particular bars 13–14 of the duet). Coincidence?

music. For example, the melodies of 'The kingdom of this world' and 'And he shall reign for ever and ever' in the 'Hallelujah' chorus have been heard as echoes of phrases in the chorale 'Wachet auf'. If so, they are fairly distant echoes.

As well as its pre-echoes in his earlier music, *Messiah* set up post-echoes and self-quotations in his later music, too. A version of 'How beautiful are the feet' reappeared in *The Anthem on the Peace* of April 1749, and

'Hallelujah' was used whole to end another anthem anthologized from existing music, the *Foundling Hospital Anthem* of the same year. George III, no less, reported that Handel himself often played the theme of 'He trusted in God' 'on key'd instruments, as a lesson ... when, making it the subject of extempory fugue and voluntary it never failed to inspire him with the most sublime ideas and wonderful sallies of imagination'.[5]

The text of *Messiah* is in the prose of the King James Bible (unlike *Saul*, but like *Israel in Egypt*). Versifying Scripture into metrical stanzas was a key part of the Reformation ideal of making the word of God accessible – the purpose, of course, was to sing it. Psalm-books like Tate and Brady's 'New Version' of 1698, still something of a novelty when Handel arrived in England, were influential and popular. Interestingly, Handel got both types of text into one piece in his Chapel Royal anthem *As Pants the Hart*, using Tate and Brady's rhyming version of Psalm 42 for some of the choruses and arias, and the earthier 'prose' version from the *Book of Common Prayer* for the less metrically regular recitatives. Jennens, as we have seen, was content to use both types in his libretti. Handel set both beautifully.

But one of the paradoxes of Handel's genius is that, while most of his English word-setting is triumphantly successful, some of it is simply not very good. Burney and other contemporaries imply that he kept his German accent during his long sojourn in England, but he must have known that the English pronounced the word 'were' as one syllable, not two:

Examples from the autograph of Handel's approach to setting the English language.

Some of his infelicities are the result of a less than perfect match between music borrowed from earlier compositions and their new words, for example the lumpy stress on the first syllable of 'For unto us a child is born', or the long melisma on the last syllable of 'And he shall purify'. Even in newly composed music the word stress sometimes falls in unlikely places, as in the example quoted on p.48. This passage attracted editorial attempts at improvement from the outset, none entirely satisfactory.

A striking linguistic quirk in the manuscript is an apparent muddle between English and German pronunciation of 'th' (one soft, one hard), producing such weird contortions as 'strenght', 'trone', and, consistently, 'death' where he means 'dead'. In at least one place this odd habit coincides with another example of what looks like carelessness, the placing of the stress on the fourth syllable of the word 'incorruptible':

Handel's editors and publishers, starting with the very first, John Walsh, continued to wrestle with the knotty problem of how best to make words and music match, as in this example. The attempt continues.

However, we do need to be fair to Handel. Pronunciation does change. There is an example elsewhere in his oratorio output where he stresses the similar word 'inexorable' in the same way, and it is clear from the metre of the verse that this is exactly what the poet intended. Perhaps his stressing of 'incorruptible' is a now-lost alternative, not a mistake.

Similarly, there are places where we can meet Handel halfway. We could quite happily sing 'cryeth' and 'com'eth' as one syllable, as in the autograph (they are, after all, simply archaic forms of our words 'cries' and 'comes'):

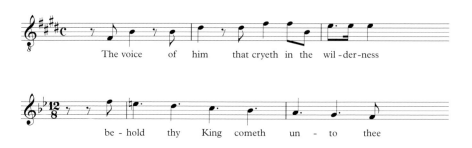

The voice of him that cryeth in the wil-der-ness

be - hold thy King cometh un - to thee

Elsewhere, Handel instinctively elided vowel-sounds between words, Italian-style:

and the glo - ry the glo -ry of the Lord

and found it entirely natural to join the first and last syllables of the word 'Halleluia' when it is repeated:

Hal - le - lu - ia Hal - le - lu - ia

William Byrd did this all the time. We don't need to add fiddly extra notes to try to pretend that they didn't.

Handel's unique approach to his adopted tongue is a fascinating and sometimes frustrating aspect of his genius, and part of what makes him the unclassifiable and endlessly absorbing character he is.

These words, lopsided stresses and all, inspired in Handel a sort of universe of musical style and form. There is something of the almost pantheistic Enlightenment embrace of writers like Addison in the reach and range of Handel's music, its internationalism, its constant reinvention of form and context, and its accumulation of brilliantly judged effects.

The instrumental 'Sinfony' which opens *Messiah* is a modified French overture, the shepherds playing the 'Pifa' or 'Pastoral Symphony' take their musical cue from their colleagues in the Abruzzo mountains outside Rome. These are common enough points of reference in the art music of the baroque.

Key relationships work within 'scenes', or groups of three or four movements. The E minor opening gives way magically to an E major *arioso* (a solo song, less formal in structure than a full aria), which halfway through turns unexpectedly into an orchestrally accompanied recitative and ends in the wrong key. It avoids any hint of monotony at the return to E major for a brief but muscular aria with the full armour of an opening and closing orchestral *ritornello*. To close the 'scene', the slab of E minor/major turns out to have been a lengthy dominant preparation for the joyous first appearance of the chorus in A major, revelling in the revelation of the Glory of the Lord. The whole scene sets a continuous passage from Isaiah, embedding textual integrity into musical logic.

As in so many of the choruses, the first musical statement of this number is given to one voice alone, in this case the altos. Handel marks this (and similar places) *tutti*, an interesting reminder that in some other places choruses would begin with a passage allocated to a soloist.

The localized organization of key groups allowed for changes when an individual item was transposed, for example the various versions of 'He shall feed his flock' in F major, B flat major or sometimes both, all of which fit neatly into their tonal surroundings. There is no attempt to plan keys over the whole 'Part' or work: Part One begins in E minor and ends in B flat major, and *Messiah* ends in D major (as it must, so the trumpets can sound in their home key).

A remarkable feature of Handel's handling of key is his use of third relationships, something we were all taught was invented by the Romantic movement and used mostly by Schubert and Jerome Kern. There is a ravishing example in 'For behold, darkness shall cover the earth', where the chromatic opening settles onto a chord of F sharp major before sliding sideways onto D major for the change of mood at 'but the Lord shall arise'. Another is the slip-sliding from C minor to A flat major between 'He trusted in God' and 'Thy rebuke', which soon wanders off into all sorts of keys (in a few bars it manages to move through F minor to E minor, finishing in B minor), in anguish matched to a sort of proto-modernist freedom of tonality like *Jephtha*'s 'Deeper, and deeper still'.

Word-painting includes wandering lines for going astray, walking in darkness and setting off for the ends of the world, the bass shaking like one of his operatic villains for the Old Testament God in his more pantomime moods, and flickering strings for angels' wings (in the autograph Handel originally marked the trumpet parts *in disparte* (off-stage) then altered this to *da lontano e un poco piano* (from a distance and fairly quietly) when the angels arrive to sing Glory to their God, but dropped the idea in the conducting score – perhaps a theatrical effect he imagined but couldn't realize).

There is some sturdy fugal stuff with a little bit of learning in the form of diminution and *stretto* (respectively, shortening the note-values in a theme and combining the theme with itself in close imitation, both tricks a well-schooled baroque musician would have imbibed from teachers and treatises at an early age), but the choral writing is generally light and clear. It's interesting to note that the choruses based on the Italian duets largely maintain the two-part texture for their contrapuntal working-out, enjoying the possibilities of a well-worked subject and counter-subject. Some of the finest moments in these movements occur when Handel adds new ideas, deliberately chordal to contrast with the aerated two-voice counterpoint, creating a thrilling moment of contrast with the clarity and light-footedness around it: 'that they may offer unto the Lord' in the chorus 'And he shall purify', and (of course) 'Wonderful, Counsellor, the mighty God' in 'For unto us a child is born'.

Part of the effect here comes from Handel's brilliant husbanding of his modest orchestral resources: trumpets and drums carefully shepherded within and between movements (as he did also in the coronation anthems), and brilliantly detailed writing for strings, full of unusual and expressive slurrings, markings and part-crossings. Bassoons would normally double the instrumental bass-line: oboes were only used by Handel from the 1743 London performances on. Neither have independent music of their own, simply doubling voices and strings. These modest but flexible requirements have contributed both to the universality and the practicality of this wonderful work over the centuries.

The solo writing, too, reveals a remarkable clarity of texture. Handel often chose to write for just voice and continuo bass, with or without an obligato instrumental line, so that just two or three musical lines are heard: sometimes just one. Handel's unsurpassable purity of line is allowed to shine, unencumbered by unnecessary harmonic filling.

The church anthem style is here, with a hint of the *canto fermo* manner (where a tune in long notes is counterpointed with faster music in other parts) in the 'Hallelujah'. The breathless hush of a choir singing 'Since by man came death' unaccompanied was something Handel's audience would

A page in Handel's own handwriting from the beautiful conducting score, copied largely by J.C. Smith, but annotated by Handel with names of soloists and changes to the music for his various performances. This evocative pair of volumes is known as the Tenbury manuscript as it spent many years in the library of St Michael's College, Tenbury Wells, Worcestershire, which was founded by Sir Frederick Ouseley in 1856. He was given the manuscript in 1867 and, along with most of the rest of the Tenbury Collection, it is now in the Bodleian Library, Oxford. MS. Tenbury 346, fol. 66r.

simply never normally have heard (a magical effect which, interestingly, he used in other works to mark the solemn moment of death).

Opera certainly gets a bow, though the full *da capo* aria appears sparingly, at moments of drama and emotional intensity like 'He was despised' and 'The trumpet shall sound'. More often, structural expectations are dashed in pieces or changed in the twinkling of an eye, like the bass being cut off from his repeat of 'Why do the nations' by the chorus piling in with its pealing demand 'Let us break their bonds asunder', a marvellously theatrical moment.

The *ritornello* aria is here, but transformed: the opening *ritornello* of 'I know that my redeemer liveth' features three or four little motifs in the violins, which reappear to duet with the voice, according to established formal practice. Between these episodes, the opening phrase returns in various keys, which again is textbook stuff: but Handel gives these statements to the singer, not just to the *obligato* violins, so as well as the tune we hear the opening words several times over: form transformed to give a calm emphasis to the sure and certain statement of faith.

Perhaps this is where we come closest to Jennens, a man whose deeply held traditions of churchmanship 'cherished a belief system based on the concept of mystery and revelation, at the centre of which stood the figure of Christ the Redeemer',[6] in the perceptive words of Jonathan Keates. Jennens himself might have been thinking of this moment when he said 'everything that has been united with Handel's music becomes sacred by such a union in my eyes'[7] (though of course he wasn't always as polite about Handel's efforts as that).

Messiah, according to Charles Burney, is 'a most happy and marvellous concatenation of harmony, melody, and great effects'.[8] And, he should have added, of words, whether Handel knew how to pronounce them or not.

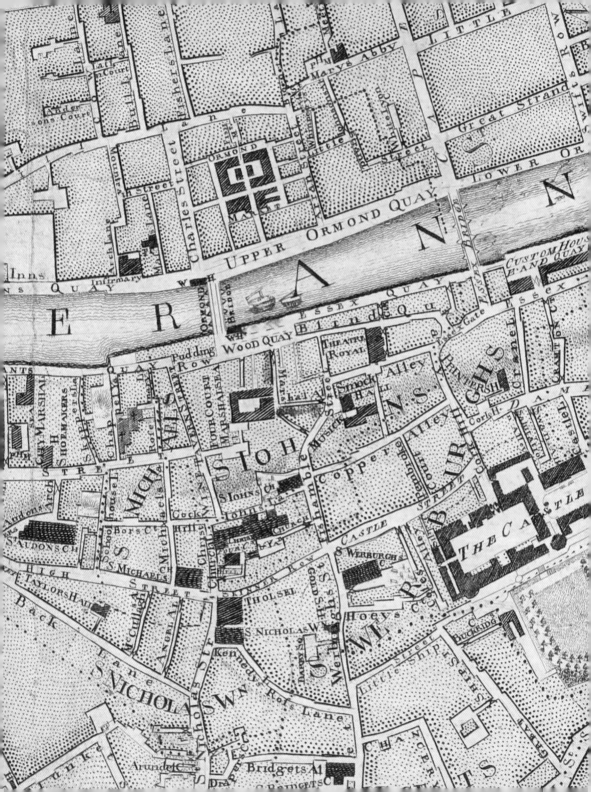

5

'FOR THIS MAY ALL YOUR SINS BE FORGIVEN'
The Dublin premiere

It is not quite clear exactly how *Messiah* came to be performed for the first time in Dublin.

On 10 July 1741 Jennens told Holdsworth that he hoped Handel would 'perform it for his own Benefit in Passion Week',[1] that is, during the regular oratorio season in London in Lent. On 2 December the same year Jennens wrote again to Holdsworth, a touch tetchily:

> I heard with great pleasure at my arrival in Town, that Handel had set the Oratorio of Messiah; but it was some mortification to me to hear that instead of performing it here he was gone into Ireland with it. However, I hope we shall hear it when he comes back ...[2]

On 29 December Handel wrote emolliently to Jennens from Dublin about 'Your Oratorio Messiah, which I set to Musick before I left England',[3] which fits with the date of composition on the autograph manuscript.

In early April the following year *Faulkner's Dublin Journal* proudly stated that the composer wrote the piece specifically for the benefit of Mercer's Hospital in the city: 'this Noble and Grand Charity for which this oratorio

Detail from John Rocque's map of 1757 showing the Music Hall on Fishamble Street, Dublin.

J. Tudor delin.

A Prospect of the CITY of DUBLIN, from the Magazine Hill, in he
Majesty's Phænix Park.

London, Printed for Rob.ᵗ Sayer Map & Prints

J. Mason sculp.

üe de la VILLE de DVBLIN de dessus l'Arsenal desu Majesté buti sur la
Montágne des Phœnix Parc.

ten Buck near Serjeants Inn, Fleet Street.

was composed'.[4] There is a touch of the blarney about this claim – although some of his music had been performed to raise money for Mercer's charity, there is no evidence that Handel had this purpose in mind when he wrote *Messiah* back in London the previous summer. Like all his large-scale pieces, *Messiah* was written to go 'into the bank' for a season whose details would emerge as circumstances required.

The immediate trigger for his decision to travel also remains a little hazy. In February 1741/2 another newspaper stated that 'the famous Mr. Handel ... had been lately invited into this Kingdom, by his Grace the Duke of Devonshire ... for the Entertainment of the Nobility and Gentry'.[5] But the status of this invitation remains a little vague. Handel must have sought, and received, Devonshire's approval for the plan, if nothing else so that he could claim that 'My Lord Duc the Lord Lieutenant ... is allways present with all His Family'[6] at his concerts, an important selling point among the 'Nobility and Gentry'.

But Handel famously made his own decisions. It seems most likely that the trip to Dublin was essentially a speculative venture. He was already well acquainted with a number of able musicians who had successfully crossed the Irish Sea. He had an established reputation to build and capitalize on: the *Dublin Journal* announced the advent of

the celebrated Dr Handell, a Gentleman universally known by his excellent Compositions in all Kinds of Musick, and particularly for his *Te Deum, Jubilate, Anthems,* and other Compositions in Church Musick, (of which for some Years past have principally consisted the Entertainments in the Round Church, which have so greatly contributed to support the Charity of Mercer's Hospital) to perform his Oratorios ...[7]

PREVIOUS PAGES
A contemporary view of Dublin, 'one of the finest and largest Cities of Europe',
as John Rocque described it. James Mason (1710–1783), after an unknown artist,
A Prospect of the City of Dublin, from the Magazine Hill, in his Majesty's Phoenix Park.

(though the writer shows the journalist's eternally cavalier attitude to accuracy by anointing him 'Dr'). The great and the good were keen to flutter round his flame: 'Mr Putland, Dean Owen & Docr Wynne be & are hereby desir'd to wait on Mr Handel & ask the favour of him to play on the Organ ...'[8]

Handel recognized the potential of the Dublin market, writing to Jennens from London on 9 September 1742, after his return home, 'Certain it is that this time 12 month I shall continue my Oratorio's in Ireland, where they are going to make a large Subscription already for that purpose.'[9] He did not, in the event, return to Dublin, but the picture of an emerging market is reinforced by the visits, both before and after Handel, of the various musical members of the Arne family (in all their complex relations), who set about 'developing the market which Handel had opened up',[10] in the words of the historian Richard Luckett. This feeds into *Messiah*, too.

Handel's sailing from Parkgate to Dublin in November 1741 was delayed by unfavourable weather. He spent the lay-off in Chester. The fifteen-year-old Charles Burney, already a convinced Handelian, was at school in the city, and remembered 'seeing him smoke a pipe, over a dish of coffee, at the Exchange-Coffee-House'. Burney related that Handel had with him some newly copied part-books for use in Ireland, and asked Mr Baker, the local organist, to gather a few singers together to read them over. They included a 'good base' called Janson who, in the immemorial custom of many cathedral lay-clerks, held down a day job as a printer. 'A time was fixed for this private rehearsal,' Burney recalled, '... but, alas! On trial of the chorus in the Messiah *"And with his stripes we are healed"* — Poor Janson, after repeated attempts, failed so egregiously, that HANDEL let loose his great bear upon him; and after swearing in four or five languages, cried out in broken English: "You shcauntrel! Tit you not dell me dat you could sing at soite?" "Yes, sir," says the printer, "and so I can, but not at *first* sight."'[11]

Burney was writing many years later, and doesn't claim to have been present. His transliteration of Handel's accent perhaps implies a certain

S^r   Dublin Decemb^r 29. 1741.

It was with the greatest Pleasure I saw the Continuation
of Your Kindness by the Lines You was pleased to send me, in
Order to be prefix'd to Your Oratorio Messiah, which I set
to Musick before I left England. I am emboldned, Sir,
by the generous Concern You please to take in relation to my
affairs, to give You an Account of the Success I have met here.
The Nobility did me the Honour to make amongst themselves
a Subscription for 6 Nights, which did fill a Room of
600 Persons, so that I needed not sell one single Ticket at the door.
and without Vanity the Performance was received with a
general Approbation. Sig^{ra} Avolio, which I brought with
me from London pleases extraordinary, I have form'd an
other Tenor Voice which gives great Satisfaction, the Bases
and Counter Tenors are very good, and the rest of the Chorus
Singers (by my Direction) do exceeding well, as for the Instruments

---

Handel's courteous and professional letter to his librettist, Jennens, dated 29 December 1741. The composer
is clearly excited by his reception in Dublin and tactfully refers to 'your Oratorio Messiah'.

inventive creativity at work. But it's a good story, and if it is true, at least in essentials, it confirms that Handel had at least some of the performing material of *Messiah* with him (perhaps hurriedly copied in London by Smith and his minions), and has the distinction of being the very first time any of the music of the oratorio was heard live, Janson's wrong notes and all. We should probably remember poor old Baker, who was not only shown up in front of his celebrity guest, but also had to work with a bass lay-clerk who could sing but not sight-read – the choirmaster's curse throughout all ages.

Handel finally arrived in Dublin on 18 November 1741.

The cast of characters who helped him make *Messiah* were a colourful crew. At the head of polite society was Devonshire, whose 'outside was unpolished, his inside unpolishable. He loved gaming, drinking, and the ugliest woman in England, his Duchess', who was 'delightfully vulgar',[12] according to Walpole in full flow and fine form. Senior clerics included Dean Cobbe of Christ Church, his counterpart at St Patrick's, the brilliant but increasingly insane Jonathan Swift, and Swift's long-suffering and music-loving chancellor, Dr Delany. Their joint cathedral choirs seem to have been pretty good, though not immune to the prevailing problems of lack of discipline and plurality – most of the lay-clerks doubled up in both places, as indeed was common practice back in London.

Among his soloists, Handel expressly 'brought over several of the best performers in the Musical Way',[13] as one newspaper reported, including the hard-working and suitably foreign-sounding soprano Christina Maria Avoglio, 'whom I brought with me from London',[14] as Handel told Jennens. The other soprano was possibly a shadowy figure called Mrs Maclaine, who was probably the wife of an itinerant Scottish organist and fiddle player, but has otherwise left little trace, despite having revealed to the world some of the most celebrated soprano music of all time. In December came Susannah Cibber, actress, sister of composer Thomas Arne and wife of actor–manager Theophilus Cibber, who had recently sued her lover using evidence obtained by means of spy holes drilled through a wainscot by a landlady and recounted in court in pornographic detail. She came to Ireland to sing in her brother's hugely successful masque *Comus* (and probably to distance herself from her recent past, dodgy even for an actress), replacing her stage rival Kitty Clive. Both are significant names in the story of *Messiah*.

Handel's male soloists were far more boringly respectable: cathedral lay-clerks William Lamb and Joseph Ward (altos), tenors James Baileys (who had sung for Handel in London) and (possibly) John Church, and basses John Hill and the former Chapel Royal choirboy John Mason. Some of the exact detail of who sang what and when remains conjecture, reconstructed from names scribbled in the score by the composer, newspaper reports, word-books annotated by audience members and other clues. Such is often the case within Handel's busy and fast-moving company of musical *confrères*. First among his instrumentalists was the fine violinist Matthew Dubourg, another seasoned Handelian from London.

Messiah was first performed in a 'Musick-Hall'. The significance of this lies in the ongoing ambiguity around oratorio: neither a concert in a church, nor the sacred in a theatre, it was a neat solution which drew the sting of potential objections from both sides. Purpose-built music rooms, the first of their kind in the world, testified to the increasingly central place of music in society. Their egalitarian atmosphere lingers in the high, white halls of the Assembly Rooms in Newcastle or the smaller spaces of the Holywell Music Room in Oxford: plain, light, with good acoustics and bad seating – perfect for concentrating on music. There was far less social division of the audience than in the theatre (and, indeed, in church).

The 'New Musick-Hall in Fishamble Street' was designed by Captain Richard Castle (yet another German immigrant in this story), skilfully

Jonathan Swift, the brilliant but increasingly erratic Dean of St Patrick's Cathedral, Dublin. Portrait by Charles Jervas, c.1718.

Swift D.D

shoehorned onto an irregular site at the bottom of a twisty hill near the Liffey. It was sometimes known as 'Neale's Musick-Hall' after the music seller who acted as treasurer for subscriptions to its construction, completed just a few weeks before Handel arrived in late 1741.

Handel's Irish venture didn't begin with *Messiah*. A six-night season starting at the end of December, featuring Avoglio and others in *L'Allegro, il Penseroso ed il Moderato* alongside a number of concertos 'did fill a Room of 600 persons ... The Audience being composed (besides the Flower of Ladyes of Distinction and other People of the greatest Quality) of so many Bishops, Deans, Heads of the Colledge, Auditor General, &tc,' as Handel reported with some satisfaction to Jennens, adding tactfully 'all of which are very much taken with the Poetry'.[15] Five more concerts followed in January. February saw two performances of the seemingly infinitely adaptable *Esther*. In March came *L'Allegro* once more, then Susannah Cibber's first recorded performance for Handel, in an English version of his penultimate opera *Imeneo*, recast as a 'serenata', a kind of less operatic opera.

Then, in late March 1741/2, came an announcement in the papers:

For Relief of the Prisoners in the several Gaols, and for the Support of Mercer's Hospital in Stephen's Street, and of the Charitable Infirmary on the Inns Quay, on Monday 12th April, will be performed at the Musick Hall in Fishamble Street, Mr Handel's new Grand Oratorio, call'd the MESSIAH, in which the Gentlemen of the Choirs of both Cathedrals will assist, with some Concertoes on the Organ, by Mr Handell. Tickets to be had at the Musick Hall, and at Mr Neal's in Christ-Church-Yard, at half a Guinea each. N.B. No Person will be admitted to the Rehearsal without a Rehearsal Ticket, which will be given gratis with the Ticket for the Performance when pay'd for.[16]

Susannah Cibber, celebrated actress, member of two famous families, and one of Handel's favourite singers. Portrait by Thomas Hudson, 1749.

As usual, patrons could also purchase their own copy of the word-book to study in advance and follow in performance: price 'a British Sixpence' (currency, not for the last time, standing proxy for the imperfect union of neighbour nations).

Things were still not completely straightforward. In January Swift had stated the usual decanal objections to his lay-clerks taking part in performances of this kind in his own inimitable style:

> whereas it hath been reported that I gave a license to certain vicars to assist at a club of fiddlers in Fishamble Street, I do hereby declare that I remember no such license to have been ever signed or sealed by me; and that if ever such pretended license should be produced, I do hereby annul and vacate the said license; intreating my said Sub-Dean and Chapter to punish such vicars as shall ever appear there, as songsters, fiddlers, pipers, trumpeters, drummers, drum-majors, or in any sonal quality, according to the flagitious aggravations of their respective disobedience, rebellion, perfidy and ingratitude ...[17]

Fortunately this splendid rant appears not to have been enacted, and the cathedral singers were able to add their 'sonal quality' to the expected *Messiah*.

Fixing and announcing the date of the first rehearsal were delayed because Susannah Cibber had been ill and had to make up some contracted performances in a play. On 3 April, the public rehearsal was advertised for the 8th, and eventually took place on the 9th. Unlike the evening subscription concerts, the performances (and presumably the rehearsals) of *Messiah* took place at noon.

Doors opened at 11.00am. The *Dublin Journal* stated unequivocally that 'Mr Handell's new Grand Sacred Oratorio, called, The MESSIAH ... gave

The rather unprepossessing entrance to the Music Hall in Fishamble Street, Dublin, where *Messiah* was first performed, recreated in this watercolour by Pauline Scott.

MUSICK HALL

THOS KENNAN.

Pauline Scott

universal Satisfaction to all present; and was allowed by the greatest Judges to be the finest Composition of Musick that ever was heard.' For the official first performance (pushed back one day to Tuesday 13th), it requested 'a Favour, that the Ladies who honour this Performance with their Presence would be pleased to come without Hoops, as it will greatly encrease the Charity, by making Room for more company'.[18] A follow-up added, in a spirit of equality, 'Gentlemen are desired to come without their Swords.'[19]

The size and composition of Handel's choir for the Dublin performances has to be inferred from the available evidence: perhaps ten or twelve men drawn from the still-active members of the two cathedral choirs, together with the three soprano soloists and possibly one or two more sopranos known to Handel from the Dublin scene. There is no direct evidence that boys from the cathedrals took part alongside their adult colleagues. The orchestra probably featured neither oboes nor bassoons. He seems to have had the pick of the players: in March a rival promoter complained of 'all the best Musick being engaged to Mr Handel's concert'.[20]

The performance is part of musical history. As so often, that history may be part mythology. Delany will forever be immortalized as the man who cried out 'Woman, for this be all thy sins forgiven thee' when Mrs Cibber sang 'He was despised'. Maybe he did. There were certainly plenty of sins to forgive. Delany was known as an impulsive and sometimes imprudent man. The oft-cited source of the story is Thomas Sheridan, who is said to have been sitting next to Delany at the time. Sheridan certainly wrote about Susannah Cibber's performances much later, but the exact provenance of the story remains hazy.[21]

What is not in doubt is the impact of that first performance. The newspapers competed with each other 'to express the exquisite Delight it afforded to the admiring crouded Audience', and praised not just Handel but Dubourg and all the adult singers for donating their fee to the three beneficiary institutions, 'satisfied with the deserved Applause of the Publick, and the

The elegant interior of the Music Hall, Dublin.

conscious Pleasure of promoting such useful, and extensive Charity'.[22]

Bishop Edward Synge gave a detailed and technically expert critique, calling it 'a Species of Musick different from any other', and focusing like many of his profession on the serious nature of the entertainment: 'tho' the young & gay of both Sexes were present in great numbers, their behaviour was uniformly grave & decent, which Show'd that they were not only pleas'd but affected with the performance. Many, I hope, were instructed by it, and had proper Sentiments inspir'd in a Stronger Manner on their Minds.'[23]

On 22 May Handel gave *Saul*, with concertos: a far bigger undertaking than the modest *Messiah*, whose second public rehearsal and performance followed on 1 and 3 June. Subscribers were told that 'This will be the last Performance of Mr Handel's during his Stay in this Kingdom.'[24]

So it proved. He paid a farewell visit to poor, mad Swift, who had begun to fulfil his own unbearably poignant prediction that 'I shall be like that tree: I shall die from the top',[25] but could barely be made to understand who his visitor was; the servant admitted him 'just to let Mr *Handel* behold the Ruins of the greatest Wit that ever lived'.[26]

Handel headed home on Friday, 13 August 1742, well and deservedly pleased with 'my Success in General in that generous and polite Nation.'[27]

6

HANDEL'S PERFORMERS AND PERFORMANCES

The popular success of the Dublin performances was not repeated in London, at least not initially. A significant factor in the cool reception was the ongoing squeamishness about singing the sacred to the kind of music more associated with the opera than the church. Opponents particularly objected to Holy Writ being sung in the secular setting of a theatre, but it was thought equally inappropriate to sing oratorios in church.

Jennens captured the point in his usual testy fashion: 'What adds to my Chagrin is, that if he makes his Oratorio ever so perfect, there is a clamour about Town, said to arise from the B[isho]ps, against performing it.'[1]

Handel leased the Covent Garden theatre for a season of oratorios in Lent 1742/3: *Samson, L'Allegro* and the *Ode on St Cecilia's Day*; then, advertised for 23 March, 'A New Sacred Oratorio. With a *Concerto* on the *Organ*. And a Solo on the Violin by Mr. *Dubourg*'.[2] Jennens reported:

> Messiah was perform'd last night, & will be again to morrow, notwithstanding the clamour rais'd against it, which has only occasion'd it being advertis'd without it's Name; a Farce, which gives me as much offence as anything

The beautiful theatre in Covent Garden, London, opened by John Rich in 1737, where Handel often performed *Messiah*. This view was painted shortly before the building was destroyed by fire in 1808.

relating to the performance can give the Bs. & other squeamish People. 'Tis after all, in the main, a fine Composition, notwithstanding some weak parts, which he was too idle & too obstinate to retouch, tho' I us'd great importunity to perswade him to it. He and his Toad-Eater Smith did all they could to murder the Words in print; but I hope I have restor'd them to Life, not without much difficulty.[3]

The alternative title *Sacred Oratorio* appeared in a variety of notices and advertisements, seemingly more or less interchangeably with *Messiah* (or *the Messiah*, or *The Messiah*, or even *Messia*); sometimes both were used in the same publication. This slightly haphazard usage supports the inference that the change of title was as much carelessness and inconsistency as theological nicety: after all, *Sacred Oratorio* is surely a more provocative title than *Messiah*.

The newspaper *The Universal Spectator* thundered into the fray: 'An *Oratorio* either is an *Act of Religion*, or it is not: if it is one I ask if the *Playhouse* is a fit *Temple* to perform it, or a Company of *Players* fit *Ministers* of *God's Word*.'[4] The writer signed himself Philalethes, 'lover of truth', a common enough type of journalistic pseudonym.

The debate was joined:

Wrote extempore by a Gentleman, on reading the Universal Spectator.

On Mr. HANDEL'S *new ORATORIO,*
perform'd at the Theatre Royal in Covent-Garden.

Cease, Zealots, cease to blame these Heav'nly Lays,
For Seraphs fit to sing Messiah's Praise!
Nor, for your trivial Argument, assign
'The Theatre not fit for Praise Divine'.[5]

Philalethes replied:

Mistake me not, I blam'd no heav'nly Lays;
Nor *Handel*'s Art which strives a Zeal to raise,
In every Soul to sing *Messiah*'s Praise:
But if to *Seraphs* you the task assign;
Are *Players* fit for *Ministry Divine*?
Or *Theatres* for *Seraphs* there to sing,
The holy Praises of their Heav'nly King?[6]

Philalethes lost this particular war of words. Handel had no difficulty getting the necessary licences to perform his sacred oratorios in the theatre in Lent, and his audiences carried on turning up without apparent concern for their worldly reputation or their immortal souls.

The Lent oratorio seasons moved gradually towards a pattern following the template of 1742/3. *Messiah* earned a regular place slowly, slotted in alongside each season's new works and revivals and revisions. Handel planned six performances in 1742/3 but gave only three, and none at all in 1744, to Mrs Delany's repeated disappointment: 'We went together last night to Joseph. 'Twas the last night, and I think I prefer it to everything he has done, except the Messiah';[7] 'Last night, alas! was the last night of the oratorio: it concluded with Saul: I was in hopes of the Messiah'[8] (though it was performed independently by the Academy of Antient Music). Handel gave *Messiah* twice in 1745, in a season designed to recoup some of the losses incurred by the overambitious 1744 concerts. These were theatre performances, in Covent Garden and the King's Theatre, Haymarket.

Various revisions came in as *Messiah* matured in its maker's mind and his soloists shifted around. The chorus was very probably the Chapel Royal boys plus the men of the main London cathedral choirs: in 1744 Handel told Jennens he wanted 'Mr Gates with his Boye's and several of the best Chorus Singers from the Choirs'[9] for his oratorio season, and it seems that he got them: Smith referred to 'the choir and boy's'[10] in oratorio, and the Earl of

The spacious and salubrious buildings of Thomas Coram's Foundling Hospital, with open fields beyond.

Shaftesbury reported 'wee had al the boys from the chapell, and abundance of other voices to fill up'[11] at a performance of *Deborah*.

Messiah was then not heard in London for three years. Covent Garden performances followed in four consecutive seasons from 1747/8.

May 1749 was a significant moment in the history of *Messiah*. Handel was asked to put on a fundraiser for Thomas Coram's new Foundling Hospital for 'the reception, maintenance and education of exposed and deserted young children'.[12] He accepted an invitation to become a governor of the charity, and on 27 May gave a concert including the *Anthem on the Peace* and the *Foundling Hospital Anthem*, both of which recycled music from *Messiah* (among other things).

The next season a plan for Handel to inaugurate the Hospital chapel's new organ failed because the organ builder hadn't finished it (not unreasonably given the tight timescales). So Handel offered *Messiah* instead: easy enough since he had given it at Covent Garden a couple of weeks earlier. The first Foundling Hospital *Messiah*, on 1 May 1750, attracted 'an infinite crowd of coaches' carrying 'a very numerous audience, who expressed the greatest satisfaction'.[13] It was repeated on 15 May. The hospital benefited to the tune of over £1,000. A pleasing pattern of popular performance and charitable benefit had begun.

Then 1751 saw a performance at the Foundling Hospital, but not at Covent Garden where the oratorio season was curtailed by the death of the Prince of Wales. Thereafter, every year from 1752 until his death, Handel presented *Messiah* both at Covent Garden and at the Foundling Hospital.

Handel's other late oratorios suffered from fashionable fickleness. Not *Messiah*. It quickly revealed its unique and seemingly eternal box-office appeal, which 'made amends for the solitude of his other oratorios',[14] as Catherine Talbot commented rather ungenerously in 1756. It also made the Foundling Hospital a great deal of money: minutes record the 'great benevolence'[15] of not just Handel but Gates and others in repeatedly donating their fees.

The creeping onset of blindness slowed Handel's work from 1751 – 'How dark, O Lord, are thy decrees' sang the chorus in *Jephtha*, written that year, echoing Samson's despairing 'Total eclipse! No sun, no moon, all dark amid the blaze of noon' of a decade earlier.

In 1753 he suffered another stroke. A fellow guest at a dinner party at Jennens' London house in May 1756 found 'Handel quite Blind, but pretty cheerful',[16] playing the piano and reminiscing about his days in Italy half a century earlier.

In 1754 Handel told the Foundling Hospital trustees that 'on account of his health, he excused himself from giving any further instructions relating to the Performances' and 'approved of the Committee's appointing Mr. Smith organist to the Chapel to conduct his Musical Compositions'.[17]

From this point it is unclear to what extent Handel took an active part in the performances. A minute of May 1757 refers to a performance 'under the direction of Mr. Handel', and advertisements continued to make the same claim right up to his death,[18] but such direction could have been more or less passive and supervisory. John Christopher Smith (junior) seems to have been in practical charge of the Foundling *Messiah* performances (and much else) for the last five years of Handel's life, and indeed beyond.

The year 1754 also saw an unfortunate little quarrel about whether Handel intended 'securing his Oratorio of Messiah to the Hospital, and that it should be performed nowhere else'[19] under the terms of his will. It turned out he did not, but it all seems to have been settled in a commendably businesslike fashion. A codicil drawn up in August 1757 bequeathed 'a fair copy of the Score and all Parts of my Oratorio called The Messiah to the Foundling Hospital'.[20]

Aside from his own performances, *Messiah* spread fairly slowly around the country in Handel's lifetime. The first performance outside London was in Oxford in 1749, and it was the mid-1750s before performances became at all widespread, exclusively (it seems) in cathedral cities, regional centres of the oratorio craze. Dublin got its annual *Messiah* before London.

The performers who carried *Messiah* out into all lands were a varied crew. Kitty Clive came from the same background as her stage sister and rival Susannah Cibber – actress, ballad singer, 'a better romp than any I ever saw'[21] according to Dr Johnson, and a fiery 'mixture of combustibles'[22] in the words of one of her theatre managers. She was light of voice and musical learning: Thomas Arne once publicly put her over his knee and spanked her

The Foundling Hospital chapel. This image dates from around 1808 (from Pyne's *Microcosm of London*). The imposing three-decker pulpit was added in the later eighteenth century. The children can be seen grouped around the organ in the large gallery. The organ shown here replaced the one given by Handel.

because she couldn't get the notes right, and Burney, a better-behaved but equally fastidious musical critic, found her singing 'intolerable'.[23] Handel clearly didn't agree.

Italians continued to feature in the higher registers, notably the long-serving soprano Signora Frasi and alto Signora Galli, joined later by other compatriots such as Passerini (recommended to Handel by his old friend Telemann). Interestingly, a soprano part-book survives with the words of one of the coronation anthems written out in phonetic pronunciation, probably, from the spelling, for an Italian: 'Mai hart is indeitin' of e gut matter' – this probably dates from the anthem's inclusion in the theatre performances of *Esther* in May 1732. The French soprano Élisabeth Duparc went under the name of 'La Francesina', which means 'the Frenchwoman' in Italian; a neat indication of the indeterminately exotic nature of these singers.

Notable among the Italian imports was Gaetano Guadagni, an elegant castrato who, Burney later wrote, was 'full of grace and propriety' with an 'artful manner of diminishing the tones of his voice like the dying notes of an Aeolian harp'.[24] Guadagni joined Handel's company in 1750, and stayed only until 1753, but earned his own versions of three arias.

Handel's *Messiah* soloists got more English the lower they sang. Among his native altos were Miss Robinson, daughter of the organist of Westminster Abbey and of one of Handel's earliest and starriest English sopranos, and, later, Miss Cassandra Frederick and Miss Isabella Young (the latter becoming Mrs Scott in 1757). His tenors and basses were almost exclusively Chapel Royal men, well-paid professional singers who trod the boards of stage and festival in addition to their regular employment in the choir stalls. John

Kitty Clive, celebrated actress and one of the soprano soloists in the first London *Messiah*, in which her stage rival Susannah Cibber sang alto. Portrait by Willem Verelst, 1740.

Beard had the distinction of singing for Handel both as a treble and as his favourite tenor (apparently going straight from one to the other in the same season, aged around seventeen), though never a full adult member of the Chapel Royal. A later writer praised Beard's 'superior conduct, knowledge of music and intelligence', adding 'he let his own discretion be the tutor and held the mirror up to nature'.[25] Handel's other tenor, Thomas Lowe, had 'the finest tenor voice I ever heard' (said Burney), but 'could never be safely trusted with anything more than a ballad, which he constantly learned by ear'.[26] Again, if Burney's comment can be believed, it is interesting to note that Handel seems to have valued these qualities of natural vocal simplicity and integrity more than great learning and sophistication. Principal basses were Henry Reinhold, sometimes also referred to as Thomas, another German-born immigrant who was the first Dragon in Lampe's *The Dragon of Wantley*; Robert Wass, a member of the choirs of St Paul's Cathedral, Westminster Abbey and the Chapel Royal all at the same time, who took over on Reinhold's death in 1751; William Savage, like Gates a bass doubling up as choirmaster, in his case at St Paul's; and Samuel Champness ('competent, but not inspired'[27] – Luckett). There was a pronounced sliding scale of fees commanded by these singers – in 1754, for example, Frasi got £6 6s. 6d., Wass £1 11s. 6d., the others somewhere between.

The Chapel Royal also provided Handel with the basis of his chorus, and, in a generous gift to what Richard Luckett memorably calls the later '*Messiah*-at-Christmas industry',[28] several occasions when some of the music was given to a boy (though one, 'Mr Savage's celebrated Boy',[29] came from St Paul's). These treble soloists are referred to as just 'The Boy' in both public records and Handel's jottings in his scores – presumably Gates and Savage turned up with their cohort and allocated the solos to the boy in best voice at the time. (On occasion the anonymity may have been a relief – another Chapel Royal event got the unenthusiastic write-up 'An anthem composed by Hendel for the occasion was wretchedly sung by Abbot, Gates,

Lee, Bird [Beard] and a boy').[30] Bernard Gates is one of those who provide a musical handshake across the ages – as a boy he knew Purcell and Blow, just as younger Handelians went on to work with associates of Mozart.

These were real professional musicians – competent, capable and technically well trained, perfectly willing to stand alongside the castrati, immigrants and actresses who made up Handel's varying corps of soloists.

Handel attended the Covent Garden *Messiah* on 6 April 1759, 'apparently in great suffering, but when he came to his concerto he rallied, and kindling as he advanced, descanted extemporaneously with his accustomed ability and force'.[31] After the concert he took to his bed. On Good Friday morning, 13 April, he 'took leave of all his friends', remarking that 'he had now done with the world'. The following morning he 'died as he lived, a good Christian, with a true sense of his duty to God and man, and in perfect charity with all the world',[32] according to a letter written by his friend and neighbour James Smyth to Bernard Granville, Mrs Delany's brother, all loyal Handelians to the last.

Messiah was the last music he heard.

MESSIAH

AN

Oratorio

IN SCORE

As it was Originally Perform'd.

Composed by

Mr HANDEL

To which are added

His additional Alterations.

London. *Printed by* Mess.rs Randall & Abell *Successors to the late* Mr J. Walsh *in Catharine Street in the Strand —of whom may be had the compleat Scores of* Samson. Alexander's Feast. *and* Acis & Galatea.

7

'WE SHALL BE CHANGED'
Versions and variants

One of the fascinations of *Messiah* is that it has not come down to us in a single version. The various sources provide an absorbing narrative of its evolution.

The autograph score reveals changes made during the actual act of composition. Further stages emerge from the pages of the conducting score, which shows, in the perceptive words of the scholar Watkins Shaw, 'not the state of the work at any one time, but a condition of change and growth'.[1] There are notes about clefs and keys, versions and sections crossed out, soloists' names in big letters – Handel jotted down one list of singers in red pencil, a precious indication that this group sang together, almost certainly in 1750. He used this score when he adapted some of the music for the *Anthem on the Peace* in 1749: a brief quotation of a slightly different bit of the Book of Revelation appears against the notes of the closing chorus as a laconic hint to his patient copyists.

Printed word-books provide another category of source. Some helpful concert-goers noted down names of the singers they heard in their copies.

All of this provides a way into the forensically complicated process of working out who sang what, when, why, and in what key, cross-referenced

The title page of the first published full score, 1767, with the slightly oversimplified claim to present the work 'As it was Originally Perform'd' with Handel's subsequent 'additional Alterations'.

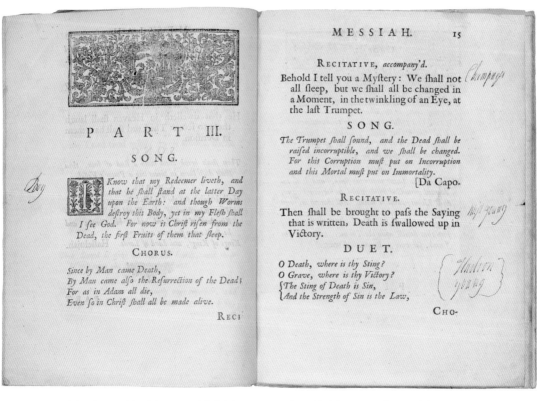

PART III.

SONG.

Know that my Redeemer liveth, and that he shall stand at the latter Day upon the Earth: and though Worms destroy this Body, yet in my Flesh shall I see God. For now is Christ risen from the Dead, the first Fruits of them that sleep.

CHORUS.

Since by Man came Death,
By Man came also the Resurrection of the Dead;
For as in Adam all die,
Even so in Christ shall all be made alive.

RECI

RECITATIVE, *accompany'd.*

Behold I tell you a Mystery: We shall not all sleep, but we shall all be changed in a Moment, in the twinkling of an Eye, at the last Trumpet.

SONG.

The Trumpet shall sound, and the Dead shall be raised incorruptible, and we shall be changed. For this Corruption must put on Incorruption and this Mortal must put on Immortality.
[Da Capo.

RECITATIVE.

Then shall be brought to pass the Saying that is written, Death is swallowed up in Victory.

DUET.

O *Death, where is thy Sting?*
O *Grave, where is thy Victory?*
{*The Sting of Death is Sin,*
{*And the Strength of Sin is the Law,*

CHO-

A London word-book from 1759. A helpful concert-goer has added the names of some of the singers, including Samuel Champness, bass, and Miss Young, alto. As was usual, the treble who sang 'I know that my redeemer liveth' is identified only as 'Boy'.

with circumstantial evidence about who was in Ireland, who was in court, and who was dead. We can watch Handel changing his *Messiah* over the eighteen years of their overlapping existence. Shaw, Larsen, Burrows, John Tobin and others have proved a formidable firm of detectives poring over the traces: a fascinating and frustrating process which reveals much but will always leave room for gaps and differences of interpretation. There is no one 'right' version of *Messiah*.

Other manuscript copies reveal Handel's intentions at any given time to a greater or lesser extent, and, indeed, the business interests of both composer and copyist. In 1756 William Hayes, Professor of Music at Oxford, wanted to borrow scores of several Handel works including *Messiah*, and was told by the Earl of Shaftesbury that 'as these have already been frequently perform'd, I can see no mateiral [*sic*] objection to doing this': but as to *Joshua* 'he will not suffer any copy to be taken or to get about from his having been in possession of the score. For otherwise both Handel and Smyth (his copiest) will be injur'd.'[2]

The score and parts bequeathed by Handel to the Foundling Hospital remain unique: the only complete (apart from a missing first soprano part) contemporary set not just of *Messiah* but of any Handel oratorio. The set must also represent the work as actually heard in a specific season at the hospital, probably 1754. On the other hand, the material was clearly never used, so any mistakes made by the (three) copyists remain uncorrected.

Printed versions existed from the very start. A good proportion of the arias (and some of the recitatives) were gradually published in vocal score between 1749 and 1759 within John Walsh's *Handel's Songs from the Latest Oratorios*, for which instrumental parts were also available for use in concerts. Walsh also issued his own arrangements like the overture 'fitted to the harpsicord or spinnet', and vocal numbers transcribed for 'German Flute, Violin or Harpsichord'. *Songs in Messiah* came out in 1763, after Handel's death, containing the overture, all the arias and some of the recits, all in full score, but no choruses. The first printed full score was issued by Randall and Abell in 1767, partly using plates engraved by Walsh over a period of decades. This of course makes it unreliable as a record of any particular performance, an issue skated over rather disingenuously in their title (see page 94).

All later editors and performers have had to face up to the fact that 'As it was Originally Perform'd' means 'as far as we know', cannot refer to any one thing, and should probably continue 'using the bits of what we know that we like and not the rest'.

Other verbal inconsistencies are clearly just mistakes: versions veer between 'And, lo' and 'But, lo' for the arrival of the angel of the Lord, and the autograph has both 'that he might deliver him' and 'would deliver him'. 'The Glory of the Lord' is given as 'the Glory of God' at one point in the first chorus. It is simple enough to mend these slips.

Rather knottier is the question of changes to the music. These are many and various. Some were made while writing: the opening of 'Thus saith the Lord', the little instrumental 'Pifa' or 'Pastoral Symphony', 'Since by man came death' and the 'Amen' all get altered, crossed out or added to actually in the autograph manuscript.

Handel's first thoughts for the fugue subject of the 'Amen' (above), and his final version (below). The revised version has more rhythmic variety, rises gratefully to the high D, and has a nice suspension built in at bars 4–5.

FACING PAGE
'How beautiful are the feet' from the Tenbury manuscript. Once again, one of Handel's soloists is identified in his big, loopy handwriting as just 'the Boy' (MS. Tenbury 347, fols 65v-66r).

'But who may abide the day of his coming? And who shall stand when he appeareth?' Two pages in
Handel's hand inserted into Smith's fair copy of the score.
(MS. Tenbury 346 fols 22v-23r)

stand when He when He appeareth and who shall stand when He app-

peareth   for He is like a refi- -ners fire and who shall stand when He

23

The awesome third-inversion dominant seventh chord, preparing the way for the ineffable pause before the last two 'Amens', was a later addition.

The autograph gives practical clues, too: the sequence of four solo numbers beginning with 'Thy rebuke' and ending with 'But thou didst not leave his soul in hell' all use the tenor clef for the vocal line. However Handel clearly regarded these as equally appropriate for a soprano, as shown by his addition of the name 'Avolio' to the score in 1743.

Other changes and evolutions can be discerned in the conducting score: the *ritornello* of 'Ev'ry valley' is pruned of an entirely redundant bar which simply repeats a pair of quavers eight times (much better made plain); 'Rejoice, greatly' began in a bucolic 12/8 version which was subsequently shortened, much to its benefit, then rewritten in 4/4 in 1745 or 1749. Several versions familiar today don't represent the composer's first thoughts: the words 'Their sound is gone out' were first included as the middle section of the first version of the aria 'How beautiful are the feet', which was itself subsequently reworked as a duet-plus-chorus; 'Thou shalt break them' was sung at the first performances as a recit, probably because the tenor couldn't manage the aria. 'And lo, the angel of the Lord' was re-composed as an aria for Kitty Clive in 1743; thereafter, Handel reverted to his original conception of this text as a colourfully accompanied recitative.

Many subsequent changes were practical, mainly to suit an individual's vocal range: '(3ʳᵈ lower A## Mr. Norris)', for example. Others were artistic, like the 1750 alto version of 'But who may abide' with its brilliant sparks flying from the refiner's fire, composed for the castrato Guadagni, replacing the original bass aria which trundles on happily in 3/8 throughout. Several solos were sung at different times by men and women. There are short sections and passages which Handel wrote and never performed.

This is the merest glimpse into the variants and versions of this mercurial masterpiece. The painstaking efforts of earlier scholars have produced comprehensive lists of what can and can't be established about what

Handel himself actually did. They make fascinating reading – and listening: a transposition gives an aria a quite different character, a musical second thought draws out different elements and emphasis of text, a shortened snatch of symphony sheds new light on the shape of a scene.

There are many surprises, and beauties, in the compositional desk drawer of Handel's *Messiah*.

8

'FOR EVER AND EVER'

The later performance history of *Messiah*

Handel went straight into the pantheon, as he knew he would: his will provided for both burial and a monument in Westminster Abbey, where he still stands in stone, peering out across the nave, clutching a page of his *Messiah*.

Hagiography can militate against accuracy. The Abbey monument had (and still has) the wrong birth date on it. John Mainwaring's *Life* of Handel, published in 1760, has the considerable distinction of being the first book-length biography of a composer ever published, but is sadly slapdash about some of the details: as well as moving Handel's death back a day so that it fell on Good Friday (as did many others), Mainwaring put the first performance of *Messiah* in London, a whole year early.

Mainwaring was also an early advocate of elevating *Messiah* to a special place not just in Handel's works but in all music, indeed in human achievement: 'favourite Oratorio', 'wonderful production', 'honour', 'magic', 'universal character'.

Performances grew along with its cult: one Leicestershire clergyman set the scene as early as September 1759 with a performance for which 'the foot-roads from every quarter were lined with common people, and the

The terracotta maquette (c.1762) by the French sculptor Louis François Roubiliac for Handel's monument in Westminster Abbey. Roubiliac and Handel moved in the same social and artistic circles: the Frenchman made his name with his other statue of Handel, for Vauxhall Pleasure Gardens.

quality and gentry in their different carriages rattled in from every part'.[1] In London, the Foundling *Messiahs* continued until 1777 (according to John Stanley), the Lent seasons to 1785, adding the names of musicians of the Mozartian generation like Thomas Linley senior and his remarkable family alongside Handelians including John Christopher Smith junior and Stanley, both of whom continued to perform *Messiah* into the 1770s.

Some writers continued to trot out the old objections to the very idea of oratorio: Dr John Brown thought Handel's librettos were 'a Degradation' (though even he had to concede that 'The *Messiah* is an Exception').[2] William Cowper observed

> Man praises man. Desert in arts or arms
> Wins public honour; and ten thousand sit
> Patiently present at a sacred song,
> Commemoration-mad; content to hear
> (Oh wonderful effect of music's power!)
> Messiah's eulogy, for Handel's sake ...
> Remember Handel?
> ... while we praise
> A talent so divine, remember too
> That His most holy book ...
> Was never meant ...
> To buckram out the memory of a man.[3]

Nobody was listening.

A couple of letters written many years apart added another notable piece to the myth-making. In 1756 Catherine Talbot noted rather vaguely that the Covent Garden audience stood for the 'grand choruses'.[4] In 1780 James Beattie reported that Lord Kinoull had told him that George II had 'happened to be present' at the first London *Messiah* (nearly four decades earlier), and had 'started up' not at the beginning of the 'Hallelujah' chorus

SUBSCRIBERS TICKET,

A ticket for the Westminster Abbey *Messiah*, 29 May 1784, part of the large-scale 'Commemoration' Festival. The festival was in fact held 99 years after Handel's birth, not 100, as the organizers apparently believed: it is not clear if the birth date on the monument in the nave, 1684, is simply wrong or uses the 'old-style' calendar in use at the time. Handel's unreliable biographer Mainwaring makes the same mistake.

but several bars in, at 'For the Lord God omnipotent reigneth'.[5] Whatever the truth of this, the habit grew: later in the century one audience member was publicly hissed for failing to get to her feet for the hallelujahs.

In 1771 a note in the Foundling Hospital accounts hinted at a trend: the chorus of thirty boys and men, already larger than Handel's own choirs, was supplemented by '26 Chorus Singers Volunteers not paid'.[6] A different kind of *Messiah* was evolving, revealed in all its full engorgement at the 1784 Commemoration performance in Westminster Abbey, part of a multi-concert Handel Festival over several days which became a regular feature of musical life at the Abbey. This *Messiah* had 500 performers including twelve trumpets, four timpani and six trombones. One awestruck listener commented that 'the effect of the first crash of such a band was astonishing', adding rather revealingly, 'They played in time – excellent time – contrary to all expectations.'[7] In a pleasing continuation of *Messiah*'s early charitable associations, the event supported the 'Fund for decay'd Musicians' (one of Handel's own charities). So did Burney's published account of the event (against his will), though, as an official record, he could not say what he really thought of 'the din and stentorophonic screams of these truly savage instruments'[8] as he later put it. He also wrote, privately, 'I dare not say what I have long thought. That it is our reverence for old authors and bigotry to Handel, that has prevented us from keeping pace with the rest of Europe in the cultivation of Music.'[9] This is an immensely perceptive comment. The addiction to a fake version of the old persisted well into the nineteenth century, and certainly contributed to the comparative lack of creative innovation in what became known as 'the land without music'.

In 1783 the actress and soprano Ann Cargill made a considerable splash with music from *Messiah* in Calcutta (where she had fled with her lover, an army officer). Jamaica heard parts of *Messiah* in the 1780s. Haydn attended the 1791 Westminster Abbey *Messiah*. America heard selections from 1770 (George Washington heard 'Comfort ye' in Boston in 1789). Accounts of subsequent performances differ in their detail, but it seems most likely that the first complete (or near-complete) American *Messiah* was the Boston

The Handel Commemoration, painted by Edward Edwards, c.1790. The view is described as 'Taken from the manager's box', looking west down the nave to where the huge band of performers is piled precariously around the organ gallery set up over the west door.

performance in 1817, which spread it over three evenings, pairing each of the three parts with the corresponding part of Haydn's *Creation*, an intriguing bit of programming. America first heard *Messiah* in a single evening the following year in Boston's Boylston Hall (at Christmas).

The European advance was led, with a neat symmetry, by Michael Arne, son of composer Thomas Arne and his wife Cecilia Young, one of Handel's favourite sopranos. Arne junior gave selections from *Messiah* in Hamburg in 1772. C.P.E. Bach presented the work complete, in German, two years later. Johann Adam Hiller staged a large-scale *Messiah* in Berlin in 1786 (sung in Italian, no doubt because many of the principal singers were Italian soloists from the Berlin opera).

The German tradition leads to one of the most intriguing incarnations of this much-travelled masterpiece, Mozart's reorchestration of 1789. The minor key music seems to have inspired his wildest reimaginings: great, thick, chromatically sliding wind chords added to the mostly unison line of 'The people that walked in darkness' make it sound like the end of *Don Giovanni*; the semiquaver figure in the opening *ritornello* of 'Thou shalt break them' is thrown on to every beat, sometimes upside down; clarinets and trombones recast *Messiah* in the sound-world of Mozart's own masses. Trumpets get a different role because of changes to the instrument and playing style. Modern ears may not agree with Mozart's commissioner, Baron von Swieten, that 'He who can clothe Handel so solemnly and so tastefully ... has felt his worth, has understood him',[10] but the result remains fascinating, odd – and funny.

The French didn't really get Handel: Berlioz referred to 'ce tonneau de porc et de bière qu'on nomme Haendel' ('this barrel of pork and beer which people call Handel').[11] Beethoven, by contrast, called Handel 'the greatest composer who ever lived'.[12]

Back in England, Handelmania made *Messiah* first choice for countless parish church organ recitals and choral festivals through the nineteenth

das Volk,_ das im Dun - keln, im Dun - keln_ wan - delt, im

Dun - keln, im Dun keln_ wan - delt, das Volk das im Dun - keln

wan - - - - - delt es sieht ein gros-ses Licht.

Handel's people walking in darkness appear to have bumped into Don Giovanni and the Commendatore: Handel's single line of music assumes an early Romantic accent in Mozart's arrangement.

A ticket for the Crystal Palace Festival performance in 1857.

century, and individual numbers rolled ceaselessly out of barrel organs and parlour pianos. At the other extreme, the big *Messiah*s carried on getting bigger. All used editions based on Mozart's 'additional accompaniments', beefed up as desired. George MacFarren added a military band to the orchestra. The apogee was reached in that temple of Victorian ingenuity, the Crystal Palace, where Sir Michael Costa conducted a choir of 2,765 and orchestra of 460 to an audience of 81,319 to mark the anniversary of Handel's death in 1859, the start of a triennial event. The *Spectator* found Sir Michael's chorus 'wonderfully grand' but in 'great confusion' in the fugues, which he should have taken 'very slow': worst of all, the solo singers were 'reduced to nothing or less than nothing ... faintly heard as it were from a great distance', sadly inevitable unless they had 'lungs of brass and a throat of iron'.[13]

Charles Dickens blamed the punters: 'People who complain that they cannot hear the solos are probably too stingy to pay for the best seats,' he wrote about the fifth triennial Festival in 1874. He found the music 'Heaven-inspired' and asked his readers to 'let Handel be our guide', even though he signed himself 'A Musical Ignoramus' and claimed to 'have no more ear for music than a lobster'.[14]

In 1906 another journalist told his readers how he 'submitted myself to the process of gradually grilling under the immense glass roof of the Crystal

A contemporary sketch of the Crystal Palace Festival, 1857, giving some idea of the vast forces involved.

Palace' but was 'well repaid' by the 'subtlety and depth' of such delights as 'Behold, the Lamb of God' 'beginning quite pianissimo', followed by a 'long drawn-out and splendidly sustained crescendo' to a 'magnificent fortissimo' before getting quiet again then ending 'on a powerful forte'.[15] It sounds positively sea-sick.

In 1891 George Bernard Shaw pointed out perceptively that all this 'dramatic expression' wilfully misrepresented what Handel had to offer: 'Why, instead of wasting huge sums on the multitudinous dullness of a Handel Festival does not somebody set up a thoroughly rehearsed and exhaustively studied performance of the Messiah in St James's Hall with a chorus of twenty capable artists? Most of us would be glad to hear the work seriously performed before we die'.[16] His instincts were shared by scholars such as Friedrich Chrysander and Ebenezer Prout, and A.H. Mann unearthed and used the Foundling Hospital material for his pioneering performances in Cambridge in 1894. Enthusiasts began collecting early instruments: by one of those pleasing coincidences in which London specializes, a notable hoard was assembled by Major Benton Fletcher in his home, Old Devonshire House, the first London residence of Handel's Lord Lieutenant of Ireland. John Tobin addressed many stylistic and logistical issues in his performances in the 1950s. In 1965 Watkins Shaw addressed head-on the knotty question: 'On what textual authority should an edition of *Messiah* rest?',[17] and set out to produce a usable answer to his own question. Modern researchers have gone further into the forensics. Their approach, appropriately, is captured with remarkable prescience by none other than Charles Jennens in his own comments about editing Shakespeare, written in 1771:

> We have never yet had a correct edition of him; there are perpetual blunders in those of the greatest authority; and in some cases we are obliged, from letters, put together, making no word, to guess the word *Shakespeare* meant. Now, though an editor, in these cases, may be allowed to conjecture, yet it is his duty to give these mutilated readings, that the public may be indulged in their conjectures, as well as himself. In this view, some readings that at present appear insignificant, may hereafter be assistant to the critical conjecturer when any new difficulties may start; and on this account an editor may not, with safety, omit any various reading, though ever so trifling; because he knows not what may, or what may not, become of use.[18]

That could have been written as a textbook approach to editing *Messiah*, with its many 'various reading[s]'.

Intriguingly, evidence about style and practice can survive in the form of a continuous performing tradition. Sir Charles Stanford heard *Messiah* in Dublin as a boy: 'Another, and to my mind very sound, Dublin tradition

Edison's phonograph in use at the 1888 Crystal Palace Festival, some of the very earliest recordings of any music. Amazingly, brief snatches of these recordings have survived and can be heard today, including music by Handel.

was the rendering of the introduction to the oratorio in *double* dots, a reading which gives far more point to the rhythm, and removes all the feeling of stodginess which a strict adherence to the printed note-values emphasizes.'[19] There speaks, perhaps, the grumpy echo of an order issued at the very first rehearsal, handed down throughout all generations.

As with editions, so with recordings. Astonishingly, one of the very earliest surviving recordings of music is a snatch of *Israel in Egypt* from the Crystal Palace Commemoration of 1888, recorded on Edison's yellow paraffin cylinder: barely audible, but recognizably capturing the actual sound of these remarkable monster performances — and clearly very well sung. Into the era of 78s and beyond, Thomas Beecham and Malcolm Sargent let us hear the echo of Crystal Palace, complete with cymbals, triangles and a *William Tell*-style *accelerando* at the end of the 'Hallelujah' from Beecham. The mid-twentieth century also gives us some fine solo singing on record from artists including Elsie Suddaby, Isobel Baillie and, a little later, Kathleen Ferrier. Later conductors like Colin Davis, Charles Mackerras and Neville Marriner brought critical intelligence to the application of authentic style to modern instruments, and began investigating Handel's variants. Donald Burrows believes that 'If we have confidence in Handel's judgement, then the best course is to pursue the plan of one of his performances in its entirety',[20] and recent notable recordings by Christopher Hogwood (with the expert choir of Christ Church Cathedral, Oxford, under Simon Preston) and Edward Higginbottom do exactly this, significantly using boys for the chorus (and, in Higginbottom's account, the solos), with revelatory results.

But, at the same time, some of what we do today is our choice, not Handel's. Do we try hard enough to match the varied vocal hinterland of Handel's solo singers? Some were operatic divas; others were balladeers and actresses. Burney said of one that her 'knowledge of musical characters was very slight';[21] of another that her voice was 'a mere thread', but with 'a natural pathos, and perfect conception of the words', which 'often penetrated the heart, when others, with infinitely greater voice and skill, could only reach the ear',[22] and elsewhere refers to the same singer's voice as 'sweet and affecting';[23] after Handel's death he praised the 'crystalline clarity'[24] of another. Who would be the modern equivalents? Should we try and imagine 'He was despised' sung by, say, Vera Lynn or Julie Andrews? What did a 'countertenor' sound like, and can his modern counterpart ever replicate the 'clear, sweet and full'[25] sound of the celebrated castrati of Handel's era? His boys' choirs were smaller (though older) than today – six boys in one Foundling chorus, just four in another. Surely this tells us something about what Swift called their 'sonal quality', which must have been pretty robust. On the other hand, Handel's soloists sang in the choruses, which today's singers would consider inappropriate.

A performance of *Messiah* in the beautiful baroque interior of the Dresden Frauenkirche in 2011,
showing how modern performance practice attempts to recreate a style
and scale of performance similar to Handel's own.

Similarly, Handel's orchestral forces are sometimes listed in detail: which minimally minded modern musicologist would use the four bassoons employed by Handel in the 1750s? Handel used horns to double his trumpets an octave lower: should we?

And, academia aside, our age is, like every other, joyously capable of recasting *Messiah* in its own image: the best of the several jazz and blues versions is, unsurprisingly, the one by Quincy Jones. Of course, Handel's subtleties disappear under the relentless rhythms as completely as they did beneath the bombast and bombazine of Crystal Palace, but the improvisatory blues style catches something intriguing in the solos, and the repeated, driving, syncopated hallelujahs make a worthy and exhilarating gospel refrain.

History goes round in circles as well as in a straight line. Perhaps if we have learned to respect the original context we must also by implication respect the context of the intervening performance history. After all, Mozart's arrangements are treated with historical deference as part of the Mozart canon. Perhaps one day someone will do a historically informed reconstruction of the Crystal Palace performance.

Messiah at Wembley?

CONCLUSION

'In the end, *Messiah* stands alone', says Donald Burrows.[1] This is a true saying. His three little opening words hint at *Messiah*'s clear-eyed look at last things and its patient gaze into the face of the eternal. '*Messiah* is, for all its lack of stated plot, a drama, though one in which the momentum is primarily internal and intellectual rather than external', adds Richard Luckett.[2] By assuming that you, the listener, know the story already it treats you as an equal, part of a shared, inclusive experience. It is not a work of dogma, but a cosmic psychodrama on themes of darkness and light, life and death. *Messiah* does not once say 'I believe'; instead it says 'I know' – and 'I know' because 'I see'. Comfort ye, my people.

Its uniqueness and ambiguity are there in its name. Is 'Messiah' an honorific, a job description, a proper name, a title, or a little bit of all of the above (and more)? Do we need to figure out our preferred answer to that question before deciding whether to award it a definite article? Handel certainly used 'Messiah' consistently. So, usually, did Jennens, though he also called it 'the Messiah' (using both in the same letter on one occasion).[3] Handel's will (written by someone else at his instruction) gives 'The Messiah'.[4] 'Messiah' must be the preferred version, as it was for composer and librettist, but the fact remains that the eighteenth century simply wasn't as bothered about standardizing such things as we are. Newspapers, music publishers and printers of promotional playbills happily switched between one and the other, and would have considered it a wholly unimportant detail.

Its ambiguity and universality are revealed, too, in how Handel used his *Messiah*. This is a work he performed in the theatre, in the music hall, and in church. Unlike us, he never performed it at Christmas, only in Lent and the period following Easter. But this was for practical and financial reasons, not liturgical: oratorios were given in Lent because the opera was closed. Handel had no difficulty with 'For unto us a child is born' being sung on Maundy Thursday (and, indeed, 'for now is Christ risen', 'Thou art gone up on high' and 'There were shepherds abiding in the field'). *Messiah* belongs to all liturgical seasons and none.

Like *Peter Pan*, its charitable associations are a key part of its hinterland. Many of Handel's associates, as well as the composer himself, regularly gave their *Messiah* earnings to charity. Burney noted how *Messiah*,

> to the honour of the public at large, and the disgrace of cabal and faction, was received with universal admiration and applause. And from that time to the present, this great work has been heard in all parts of the kingdom with increasing reverence and delight; it has fed the hungry, clothed the naked, fostered the orphan, and enriched succeeding managers of Oratorios, more than any single musical production in this or any other country.[5]

The early prohibition on hoops and swords adds to the inclusive aura of egalitarianism which hovers over the pages of the score like the wings of the angel. This is a work for 'all nations', not just the 'elect'. Charles Dickens noted that participants in the massed choir movement of the 1850s, in which *Messiah* played such a crucial part, 'belong to every class and calling; the highest ranks of the aristocracy, the members of almost every trade and profession, the industrious mechanic and workman; and they all mingle in one pursuit, without regard to station or degree, and with the utmost harmony of feeling ... [and] such uniform propriety and decorum, that the most scrupulous parents allow their children, without hesitation, to attend them'.[6] Today we have the 'scratch' *Messiah* and the 'Come-and-sing', a three-word invitation which surely sums up the inclusive joy of this work, and indeed of choral singing generally.

Like one of its characters, *Messiah* sets out to bring great joy to all people. It remains unequalled.

APPENDIX I

Jennens' scenic structure for *Messiah*

Part I

'The prophecy and realization of God's plan to redeem mankind by the coming of the Messiah'

Scene 1: 'Isaiah's prophecy of salvation' (movements 2–4)

Scene 2: 'The prophecy of the coming of Messiah and the question, despite (1), of what this may portend for the World' (movements 5–7)

Scene 3: 'The prophecy of the Virgin Birth' (movements 8–12)

Scene 4: 'The appearance of the Angels to the Shepherds' (movements 13–17)

Scene 5: 'Christ's redemptive miracles on earth' (movements 18–21)

Part II

'The accomplishment of redemption by the sacrifice of Christ, mankind's rejection of God's offer, and mankind's utter defeat when trying to oppose the power of the Almighty'

Scene 1: 'The redemptive sacrifice, the scourging and the agony on the cross' (movements 22–30)

Scene 2: 'His sacrificial death, His passage through Hell and Resurrection' (movements 31–2)

Scene 3: 'His ascension' (movement 33)

Scene 4: 'God discloses his identity in Heaven' (movements 34–5)

Scene 5: 'Whitsun, the gift of tongues, the beginning of evangelism' (movements 36–9)

CHORUS.

Their Sound is gone out into all Lands, and their Words unto the Ends of the World.

SONG.

Why do the Nations so furiously rage together, and why do the People imagine a vain thing? The Kings of the Earth rise up, and the Rulers take counsel together, against the Lord and against his Anointed.

CHORUS.

Let us break their Bonds asunder, and cast away their Yokes from us.

RECITATIVE.

He that dwelleth in Heaven shall laugh them to scorn: The Lord shall have them in Derision.

SONG.

Thou shalt break them with a Rod of Iron, thou shalt dash them in pieces like a Potter's Vessel.

CHORUS.

Hallelujah, for the Lord God Omnipotent reigneth. The Kingdom of this World is become the Kingdom of our Lord and of his Christ; and he shall reign for ever and ever.
King of Kings, and Lord of Lords. Hallelujah.

PART

PART III.

SONG.

I Know that my Redeemer liveth, and that he shall stand at the latter Day upon the Earth: and though Worms destroy this Body, yet in my Flesh shall I see God. For now is Christ risen from the Dead, the first Fruits of them that sleep.

CHORUS.

Since by Man came Death, By Man came also the Resurrection of the Dead; For as in Adam all die, Even so in Christ shall all be made alive.

RECITATIVE accompany'd.

Behold I tell you a Mystery: We shall not all sleep, but we shall be all changed in a Moment, in the twinkling of an Eye, at the last Trumpet.

SONG.

The Trumpet shall sound, and the Dead shall be raised incorruptible, and we shall be changed. For this Corruption must put on Incorruption, and this Mortal must put on Immortality. ⌊Da Capo.

RECITATIVE.

Then shall be brought to pass the Saying that is written, Death is swallowed up in Victory.

DUET.

A word-book from a performance of *Messiah* in Oxford, 1752.

Scene 6: 'The world and its rulers reject the Gospel' (movements 40–41)

Scene 7: 'God's triumph' (movements 42–4)

Part III

'A Hymn of Thanksgiving for the final overthrow of Death'

Scene 1: 'The promise of bodily resurrection and redemption from Adam's fall' (movements 45–6)

Scene 2: 'The Day of Judgement and general Resurrection' (movements 47–8)

Scene 3: 'The victory over death and sin' (movements 49–52)

Scene 4: 'The glorification of the Messianic victim' (movement 53)

APPENDIX 2

Messiah: A Sacred Oratorio
Words selected from the Scriptures by Charles Jennens

Note: where Handel set an individual number for different forces
on different occasions, the main variants are given.

Part I

1 Sinfonia (Overture)

2 Accompagnato Tenor

Comfort ye, comfort ye my people, saith your God. Speak ye comfortably to
Jerusalem, and cry unto her, that her warfare is accomplished, that her iniquity
is pardoned. The voice of him that crieth in the wilderness; prepare ye the way of
the Lord; make straight in the desert a highway for our God.
(Isaiah 40:1–3)

3 Air Tenor

Ev'ry valley shall be exalted, and ev'ry mountain and hill made low; the crooked
straight and the rough places plain.
(Isaiah 40:4)

4 Chorus

And the glory of the Lord shall be revealed, and all flesh shall see it together:
for the mouth of the Lord hath spoken it.
(Isaiah 40:5)

5 Accompagnato Bass

Thus saith the Lord, the Lord of hosts: Yet once a little while and I will shake the heavens and the earth, the sea and the dry land. And I will shake all nations; and the desire of all nations shall come. The Lord, whom ye seek, shall suddenly come to His temple, even the messenger of the Covenant, whom ye delight in; behold, He shall come, saith the Lord of hosts.
(Haggai 2:6–7; Malachi 3:1)

6 Air Alto or soprano

But who may abide the day of His coming, and who shall stand when He appeareth?
For He is like a refiner's fire.
(Malachi 3:2)

7 Chorus

And He shall purify the sons of Levi, that they may offer unto the Lord an offering in righteousness.
(Malachi 3:3)

8 Recitative Alto

Behold, a virgin shall conceive and bear a son, and shall call His name Emmanuel, God with us.
(Isaiah 7:14; Matthew 1:23)

9 Air Alto

O thou that tellest good tidings to Zion, get thee up into the high mountain. O thou that tellest good tidings to Jerusalem, lift up thy voice with strength; lift it up, be not afraid; say unto the cities of Judah, behold your god! Arise, shine, for thy light is come, and the glory of the Lord is risen upon thee.

Chorus

O thou that tellest …
(Isaiah 40:9; 60:1)

10 Accompagnato Bass

For behold, darkness shall cover the earth, and gross darkness the people; but the Lord shall arise upon thee, and His glory shall be seen upon thee. And the Gentiles shall come to thy light, and kings to the brightness of thy rising.
(Isaiah 60:2–3)

11 Air Bass

The people that walked in darkness have seen a great light; and they that dwell in the land of the shadow of death, upon them hath the light shined.
(Isaiah 9:2)

12 Chorus

For unto us a child is born, unto us a son is given, and the government shall be upon His shoulder; and His name shall be called Wonderful, Counsellor, the mighty God, the Everlasting Father, the Prince of Peace.
(Isaiah 9:6)

13 Pifa ('Pastoral Symphony')

14a Recitative Soprano

There were shepherds abiding in the field, keeping watch over their flocks by night.
(Luke 2:8)

14b Accompagnato Soprano

And lo, the angel of the Lord came upon them, and the glory of the Lord shone round about them, and they were sore afraid.
(Luke 2:9)

15 Recitative Soprano

And the angel said unto them: 'Fear not, for behold, I bring you good tidings of great joy, which shall be to all people. For unto you is born this day in the city of David a Saviour, which is Christ the Lord.'
(Luke 2:10–11)

16 Accompagnato Soprano

And suddenly there was with the angel, a multitude of the heavenly host, praising God, and saying:
(Luke 2:13)

17 Chorus

'Glory to God in the highest, and peace on earth, good will towards men.'
(Luke 2:14)

18 Air Soprano

Rejoice greatly, O daughter of Zion; shout, O daughter of Jerusalem! Behold, thy King cometh unto thee;
He is the righteous Saviour, and He shall speak peace unto the heathen.
(Zecharaiah 9:9–10)

19 Recitative Alto

Then shall the eyes of the blind be opened, and the ears of the deaf unstopped.
Then shall the lame man leap as an hart, and the tongue of the dumb shall sing.
(Isaiah 35:5–6)

20 Air (or Duet) (Alto &) soprano

He shall feed His flock like a shepherd; and He shall gather the lambs with His arm, and carry them in His bosom, and gently lead those that are with young.
Come unto Him, all ye that labour, come unto Him that are heavy laden, and He will give you rest. Take his yoke upon you, and learn of Him, for He is meek and lowly of heart, and ye shall find rest unto your souls.
(Isaiah 40:11; Matthew 11:28–9)

21 Chorus

His yoke is easy, and His burden is light.
(Matthew 11:30)

Part II

22 Chorus

Behold the Lamb of God, that taketh away the sin of the world.
(John 1:29)

23 Air Alto

He was despised and rejected of men, a man of sorrows and acquainted
with grief.
He gave His back to the smiters, and His cheeks to them that plucked off His
hair: He hid not His face from shame and spitting.
(Isaiah 53:3; 50:6)

24 Chorus

Surely He hath borne our griefs, and carried our sorrows! He was wounded for
our transgressions, He was bruised for our iniquities; the chastisement of our
peace was upon Him.
(Isaiah 53:4−5)

25 Chorus

And with His stripes we are healed.
(Isaiah 53:5)

26 Chorus

All we like sheep have gone astray; we have turned every one to his own way.
And the Lord hath laid on Him the iniquity of us all.
(Isaiah 53:6)

27 Accompagnato Tenor

All they that see Him laugh Him to scorn; they shoot out their lips,
and shake their heads, saying:
(Psalm 22:7)

28 Chorus

'He trusted in God that He would deliver Him;
let Him deliver Him, if He delight in Him.'
(Psalm 22:8)

29 Accompagnato Tenor

Thy rebuke hath broken His heart: He is full of heaviness. He looked for some to
have pity on Him, but there was no man, neither found He any to comfort him.
(Psalm 69:20)

30 Arioso Tenor

Behold, and see if there be any sorrow like unto His sorrow.
(Lamentations 1:12)

31 Accompagnato Soprano or tenor

He was cut off out of the land of the living:
for the transgressions of Thy people was He stricken.
(Isaiah 53:8)

32 Air Soprano or tenor

But Thou didst not leave His soul in hell; nor didst Thou suffer
Thy Holy One to see corruption.
(Psalm 16:10)

33 Chorus

Lift up your heads, O ye gates; and be ye lift up, ye everlasting doors; and the King of Glory shall come in. Who is this King of Glory? The Lord strong and mighty, The Lord mighty in battle. Lift up your heads, O ye gates; and be ye lift up, ye everlasting doors; and the King of Glory shall come in. Who is this King of Glory? The Lord of Hosts, He is the King of Glory.
(Psalm 24:7–10)

34 Recitative Tenor

Unto which of the angels said He at any time: '
Thou art My Son, this day have I begotten Thee?'
(Hebrews 1:5)

35 Chorus

Let all the angels of God worship Him.
(Hebrews 1:6)

36 Air Alto or soprano

Thou art gone up on high; Thou hast led captivity captive, and received gifts for men; yea, even from Thine enemies, that the Lord God might dwell among them.
(Psalm 68:18)

37 Chorus

The Lord gave the word; great was the company of the preachers.
(Psalm 68:11)

38 Air (or Duet and Chorus) Soprano or alto (or soprano, alto and Chorus)

How beautiful are the feet of them that preach the gospel of peace,
and bring glad tidings of good things.
(Isaiah 52:7; Romans 10:15)

39 Chorus (or Air for tenor)

Their sound is gone out into all lands, and their words
unto the ends of the world.
(Romans 10:18; Psalm 19:4)

40 Air (or Air and Recitative) Bass

Why do the nations so furiously rage together, and why do the people imagine a
vain thing? The kings of the earth rise up, and the rulers take counsel
together against the Lord, and against His anointed.
(Psalm 2:1–2)

41 Chorus

Let us break their bonds asunder, and cast away their yokes from us.
(Psalm 2:3)

42 Recitative Tenor

He that dwelleth in Heav'n shall laugh them to scorn;
The Lord shall have them in derision.
(Psalm 2:4)

43 Air Tenor

Thou shalt break them with a rod of iron; thou shalt dash them
in pieces like a potter's vessel.
(Psalm 2:9)

44 Chorus

Hallelujah: for the Lord God Omnipotent reigneth. The kingdom of this world is
become the kingdom of our Lord, and of His Christ; and He shall reign for ever
and ever. King of Kings, and Lord of Lords. Hallelujah!
(Revelation 19:6; 11:15; 19:16)

Part III

45 Air Soprano

I know that my Redeemer liveth, and that He shall stand at the latter day upon the earth. And though worms destroy this body, yet in my flesh shall I see God. For now is Christ risen from the dead, the first fruits of them that sleep.

(Job 19:25–6; I Corinthians 15:20)

46 Chorus

Since by man came death, by man came also the resurrection of the dead. For as in Adam all die, even so in Christ shall all be made alive.

(I Corinthians 15:21–2)

47 Accompagnato Bass

Behold, I tell you a mystery; we shall not all sleep, but we shall all be changed in a moment, in the twinkling of an eye, at the last trumpet.

(I Corinthians 15:51–2)

48 Air Bass

The trumpet shall sound, and the dead shall be raised incorruptible, and we shall be changed.
For this corruptible must put on incorruption and this mortal must put on immortality.

(I Corinthians 15:52–3)

49 Recitative Alto

Then shall be brought to pass the saying that is written:
'Death is swallowed up in victory.'

(I Corinthians 15:54)

50 Duet Alto and tenor

O death, where is thy sting? O grave, where is thy victory?
The sting of death is sin, and the strength of sin is the law.

(I Corinthians 15: 55–6)

51 Chorus

But thanks be to God, who giveth us the victory through our Lord Jesus Christ.
(I Corinthians 15:57)

52 Air Soprano

If God be for us, who can be against us? Who shall lay anything to the charge of
God's elect? It is God that justifieth, who is he that condemneth?
It is Christ that died, yea rather, that is risen again, who is at the
right hand of God, who makes intercession for us.
(Romans 8:31; 8:33–4)

53 Chorus

Worthy is the Lamb that was slain, and hath redeemed us to God by His blood, to
receive power, and riches, and wisdom, and strength, and honour, and glory, and
blessing. Blessing and honour, glory and power, be unto Him that sitteth upon
the throne, and unto the Lamb, for ever and ever. Amen.
(Revelation 5:12–14)

NOTES

Introduction

1   Robert Seymour, *A Survey of the Cities of London and Westminster*, J. Read, London, 1735, vol. II, p. 666.
2   John Rocque, *Survey of the city and suburbs of Dublin*, 1757.
3   John Locke, *The Reasonableness of Christianity*, Awnsham and Churchill, London, 1695.
4   Richard Luckett, *Handel's Messiah: A Celebration*, Harcourt Brace, London, 1992, p. 77.
5   Psalm 148, v. 12.
6   Luckett, *Handel's Messiah*, pp. 37–8.

Chapter 1

1   Letter, May 1756: see, for example, Edward Blakeman, *The Faber Pocket Guide to Handel,* Faber, London, 2011, p. 283.
2   See, for example, letter of 3 January 1749, to James Harris, quoted in David Vickers (ed.), *Handel*, Routledge, London, 2017, p. 93.
3   Two versions of this epigram are recognized as possibly authentic. This is the later but probably more reliable, taken from the collected edition of Byrom's poems, published in 1773.
4   Minutes of Royal Academy of Music directors' meeting, 30 November 1719. See *George Frideric Handel: Collected Documents*, ed. Donald Burrows, Helen Coffey, John Greenacombe and Anthony Hicks, Cambridge University Press, Cambridge, 2013, vol. 1, p. 450.
5   Handel to Jennens, 29 December 1741.
6   Donald Burrows, *Handel: Messiah*, Cambridge University Press, Cambridge, 1991, p. 61.
7   Annotation in a copy of Mainwaring's biography of Handel which apparently belonged to George III, reproduced by a later owner, William C. Smith, in 'George III, Handel and Mainwaring', *Musical Times*, vol. 65, 1924, pp. 789–95. The copy of the Mainwaring was lost in World War II. See David Hunter, *The Lives of George Frideric Handel*, Boydell, London, 2015, pp. 309–10.

Chapter 2

1   Letter to Sir Horace Mann, 24 February 1743. See, for example, R. Bentley (ed.), *The Letters of Horace Walpole, Earl of Orford, to Sir Horace Mann ...*, London, 1843, p. 262. The editor comments, 'It was customary at this time for the galleries to call for a ballad called "The Roast Beef of Old England" between the acts, or before or after the play.'

2   James Grassineau, *A Musical Dictionary; Being a Collection of Terms and Characters, as well Ancient as Modern ...*, J. Wilcox, London, 1740, p. 168; reproduced in John Arnold, *The Complete Psalmodist*, R. Brown, London, 1753.

3   *Bibliothèque Britannique, Ou Histoire des Ouvrages des Sçavans de la Grande-Bretagne*, April–June 1740, pub. 'chez Pierre de Hondt'. See Stanford University, *Handel Reference Database*, https://web.stanford.edu/~ichriss/HRD/1740.htm. The French translates as 'Oratorio is a type of opera which could be defined as sacred or spiritual opera ... the usual pomp of the theatre ... certain rules concerning the performance: oratorio allows neither theatrical costume, nor stage machinery, nor changes of scenery, nor dances, nor exits and entrances by the actors ... or singing musicians ...'.

4   'More suited to the playhouse, or a Tavern, than the church,' said John Evelyn in his diary.

5   Jens Peter Larsen, *Handel's Messiah: Origins, Composition, Sources,* second edition, Greenwood Press, London, 1990, p. 10.

6   According to Handel scholar Donald Burrows, Handel 'gave Princess Anne every opportunity to hear the best of his recent music ... and she may specifically have asked to hear [*Athalia*] ... as she had also reputedly done with "Esther" the previous year.' D. Burrows, *Handel*, Oxford University Press, Oxford, 2012, pp. 289 and 321.

7   In the anonymous satirical pamphlet 'See and Seem Blind', May 1732, pp. 14–16, quoted for example in Burrows, *Handel*, p. 217.

8   This story was quoted many decades later by the diarist Hester Thrale, who was sanguine enough to note that 'the Story is so very good & comical that I must doubt the truth of it'. See George E. Dorris, *Paolo Rolli and the Italian Circle in London 1715–1744,* Mouton and Co., The Hague, 1967, p. 101.

9   Charles Burney, *An account of the musical performances in Westminster Abbey and the Pantheon ... [May/June] 1784,* pub. 1785, pp. 100–101. See also Burney's 'Sketch of the Life of Handel' in the same volume, p. 22.

10 *The Daily Journal*, 19 April 1732, reproduced in, for example, Burrows, *Handel*, p. 212.

11 *The Oxford Act, A.D. 1733, Being a Particular and Exact Account of That Solemnity*, pub. by Wilford, London, 1735, p. 75.

12 From a pamphlet of 1733, an account of the ceremonies and performances during Handel's visit, quoted by John H. Mee in *The Oldest Music Room in Europe*, John Lane/The Bodley Head, Oxford, 1911, pp. xiii–xv.

13 Charles Jennens to Lord Guernsey, 19 September 1738.

14 Handel to Jennens, 28 July 1735.

15 An anonymous 'puffing' letter, signed 'Y.Z.', first published at the first run of *Israel in Egypt*, reprinted as an introduction to the single performance in 1740.

16 Jennens to Holdsworth, 10 July 1741.

Chapter 3

1   Letter, Jennens to Holdsworth, 5 December 1743.
2   Sermon at Jennens' funeral given by Rev. George Kelly.
3   Holdsworth (in Venice) to Jennens, 23 April 1742.
4   Jennens to Guernsey, 19 September 1738.
5   Smith, Ruth, *Charles Jennens: The man behind Handel's Messiah*, Handel House Trust Ltd, 2012, p. 67.
6   Jennens to Guernsey, 19 September 1738.
7   Handel to Jennens, 9 September 1742.
8   Jennens to Holdsworth, 30 August 1745.
9   Jennens to Holdsworth, 21 February 1742/3.
10 Jennens to Holdsworth, 17 January 1742/3.
11 Handel to Jennens, 19 July 1744.
12 Jennens to Holdsworth, 7 May 1744.
13 Watkins Shaw, *A Textual and Historical Companion to Handel's 'Messiah'*, Novello, London, 1965, p. 77.
14 Larsen, *Handel's Messiah*, pp. 210 and 323.

Chapter 4

1   Jennens to Harris, 15 January 1739/40.
2   Jennens to Holdsworth, 17 January 1742/3.
3   Donald Burrows, *Handel and the English Chapel Royal*, Oxford University Press, Oxford, 2005, p. 375.
4   Jonathan Keates, *Messiah*, Head of Zeus, London, 2016, p. 101.
5   Quoted in ibid., p. 106.
6   Ibid., p. 79.
7   Quoted in Smith, *Charles Jennens*, p. 41.
8   Burney, *An account*, p. 83.

Chapter 5

1   Jennens to Holdsworth, 10 July 1741.
2   Jennens to Holdsworth, 2 December 1741.
3   Handel to Jennens, 29 December 1741.
4   *Dublin Journal*, 10 April 1742.
5   *Pue's Occurrences*, vol. 39, no. 11, 2–6 February 1741/2
6   Handel to Jennens, 29 December 1741.
7   *Dublin Journal*, 21 November 1741.
8   Minutes of a meeting of the Governors of Mercer's Hospital, 21 November 1741.
9   Handel to Jennens, 9 September 1742.
10 Luckett, *Handel's Messiah*, p. 132.
11 Burney, 'Sketch', footnote to p. 26, in *An account*.
12 Horace Walpole, Earl of Orford, *Memoirs of the Reign of King George II*, written 1796, pub. posthumously, chap. 7.
13 *Dublin Journal*, 21 November 1741.
14 Handel to Jennens, 29 December 1741.
15 Ibid., as quoted in Burrows, *Messiah*, p. 15. See also Donald Burrows, 'A new Handel letter', *The Handel Institute Newsletter*, vol.24/1, 2013, pp. 1–2; also (with Paul Tindall) 'Gustavus Waltz: a new discovery', ibid., pp. 3–4.
16 *Dublin Journal*, 27 March 1741/2, and elsewhere with slight modifications.
17 Jonathan Swift, *An Exhortation Addressed to the Sub-Dean and Chapter of St Patrick's Cathedral, Dublin,*

28 January 1741/2, reproduced in full in, for example, Walter Scott, *The Works of Jonathan Swift*, Edinburgh, 1824, vol. 19, p. 253.

18 *Dublin Journal*, 10 April 1741.

19 Ibid., 13 April 1741.

20 Ibid., 27 February, 1741/2. The promoter was 'Monsieur de Rheiner, a distress'd foreign gentleman'.

21 Mrs Cibber's modern biographer states 'the story of Dr Delany's outburst is attributed to Thomas Sheridan, who sat next to him, but I cannot find it in his surviving work' (see Mary Nash, *The Provoked Wife: The Life and Times of Susannah Cibber*, Little, Brown, London, 1977, p. 342n.). As Nash acknowledges, the earliest printed reference to the story is in Thomas Davies, *Memoirs of the Life of David Garrick*, 1780, vol. 2, p. 111. But even here the record is not completely clear: Davies does not name Dr Delany, and attributes the outburst to 'a certain bishop', a rank which Delany never achieved. As so often, the precise details of a spoken remark passed down in oral tradition cannot be verified, and in a sense are not really the point: Davies remarks perceptively that 'though I do not vouch for the following story, yet it will serve to prove the public opinion of her musical expression'. It has been fulfilling that function for nearly three centuries.

22 *Dublin Journal*, 17 April 1741.

23 A copy of Synge's analysis in the hand of J.C. Smith senior was enclosed by Handel in his letter to Jennens of 9 September 1742.

24 *Dublin Journal*, 29 May 1741, and other dates.

25 Quoted in Thomas Archer, *The Highway of Letters and its Echos of Famous Footsteps*, Randolph, New York, 1893, p. 380.

26 Swift's housekeeper, Mrs Pilkington, quoted in Griffiths and Griffiths (eds), *The Monthly Review*, vol. 11, December 1754, p. 409.

27 Handel to Jennens, 9 September 1742.

Chapter 6

1 Jennens to Holdsworth, 21 February 1742/3.

2 *London Daily Post and General Advertiser*, 23 March 1742/3.

3 Jennens to Holdsworth, 24 March 1742/3.

4 *The Universal Spectator and Weekly Journal*, 19 March 1742/3.

5 Ibid., 16 April 1742/3.

6 Ibid., 16 April 1742/3.

7 Mrs Delany to Mrs Dewes, 15 March 1743/4.

8 Mrs Delany to Mrs Dewes, 22 March 1743/4.

9 Handel to Jennens, 9 June 1744.

10 J.C. Smith senior to James Harris, June 1744, quoted in Donald Burrows, *Chapel Royal*, p. 299.

11 Quoted in Burrows, *Chapel Royal*, p. 300.

12 The phrase is from the hospital's charter, 1739.

13 As reported by the antiquarian William Stukeley, quoted in Luckett, *Handel's Messiah,* p. 167.

14 Letter to Mrs Carter, 13 April 1756. See *A Series of Letters between Mrs Elizabeth Carter and Miss Catherine Talbot 1741–1770*, pub. J. Rivington, London, 1809, vol. II, p. 227.

15 Minutes, 18 April 1750.

16 Diary of George Harris, 29 May 1756, rep. in Smith, *Charles Jennens*, p. 46.

17 Minutes, 25 June 1754.

18 For example the notices for the performance on 18 May 1756.

19 Minutes of a subcommittee of the Foundling Hospital, 2 January 1753/4.

20 Codicil, 30 July 1757.

21 James Boswell, *The Life of Samuel Johnson*, vol. 8, p. 238 (entry for 1783).

22 Tate Wilkinson, *Memoirs of his own life*, T. and J. Egerton, London, 1790, vol. 3, p. 42.

23 Charles Burney, *A General History of Music, from the Earliest Ages to the Present Period*, London, 1776, vol. 1, p. 863.

24 Ibid., vol. 2, p. 876.

25 Quoted in Jonathan Keates in *Handel: The Man and His Music*, Hamish Hamilton, London, 1986, p. 190.

26 Charles Burney, *A General History*, vol. 4, p. 667.

27 Luckett, *Handel's Messiah*, p. 168.

28 Ibid., p. 161.

29 *Jackson's Oxford Journal*, 2 July 1757, quoted in Shaw, *Historical Companion*, Novello, London, 1965, p. 64. Savage, master of the boys at St Paul's, had sung for Handel as a boy himself.

30 Diary of the Earl of Egmont, 27 April 1736, quoted for example in Burrows, *Chapel Royal*, Oxford University Press, Oxford, 2005, p. 343.

31 *Whitehall Evening Post*, 7 April 1759 (see Keates, *Handel*, p. 308).

32 James Smyth, letter to Bernard Granville (see ibid., p. 309).

Chapter 7

1 Shaw, *Historical Companion*, p. 42.

2 Ibid., pp. 73–4.

Chapter 8

1 See Luckett, *Handel's Messiah*, p. 186.

2 See ibid., p. 85.

3 William Cowper, *The Task: A poem, in six books*, 1785, Book 6: 'The Winter Walk at Noon'.

4 Letter to Mrs Carter, 13 April 1756. See *A Series of Letters between Mrs Elizabeth Carter and Miss Catherine Talbot 1741–1770*, vol. II, p. 226.

5 Letter from Dr Beattie to Rev Dr Lang, 25 May 1780. See Sir William Forbes, *An Account of the Life and Writings of James Beattie LL.D*, Isaac Riley, New York, 1806, p. 330.

6 Burrows, *Messiah*, p. 48.

7 Keates, *Messiah*, p. 140.

8 In Abraham Rees, *The Cyclopaedia, or Universal Dictionary of Arts, Sciences and Literature*, quoted in Luckett, *Handel's Messiah*, p. 203.

9 Quoted in Luckett, *Handel's Messiah*, p. 203 and elsewhere.

10 Letter, Gottfried van Swieten to Mozart, 21 March 1789.

11 Letter to M. Bennet, Paris, 26 or 27 January 1857.

12 Speaking to J.A. Stumpff in the autumn of 1823. Published in Friedrich Kerst, *Beethoven der Mann und der Künstler, wie in seinen Eigenen Words enthüllt*, no. 112; Friedrich Kerst (trans. Henry Edward Krehbiel), *Beethoven, the Man and the Artist, as Revealed in his own Words*, Dover Publications, New York, 1964, p. 54.

13 *Spectator*, 20 June 1857, p. 10, reviewing the performance preparatory for the 1859 Festival.

14 'The Handel Festival' in *All The Year Round*, 27 June 1874.

15 'The Handel Festival: A Revelation' in *The Otago Daily Times*, 11 August 1906.

16 *The World*, 21 January 1891. As Burrows points out (*Messiah*, p. 116), Shaw elsewhere welcomes the 'mass appeal' of the large-scale performance tradition.

17 Shaw, *Historical Companion*, p. 135.

18 In Charles Jennens, *The Tragedy of King Lear, as lately published, vindicated from the abuse of Critical reviewers*, 1777, p. 11.

19 C.V. Stanford, *Pages from an Unwritten Diary*, Edward Arnold, London, 1914, p. 43, quoted in Shaw, *Historical Companion*, p. 204.

20 Burrows, *Messiah*, p. 44.

21 Burney on the soprano Giulia Frasi (his pupil), quoted in Luckett, *Handel's Messiah*, p. 159.

22 Burney on Susannah Cibber, according to his daughter Fanny in Frances Burney, *Memoirs of Doctor Burney*, Cambridge University Press, Cambridge, 2010, vol. 2, p. 899.

23 Burney on Susannah Cibber, quoted in Luckett, *Handel's Messiah*, p. 166.

24 Burney on Cecilia Linley, quoted in ibid., p. 190.

25 Burney on Guadagni, quoted in ibid., p. 166.

Conclusion

1 Burrows, *Messiah*, p. 57.

2 Luckett, *Handel's Messiah*, p. 76.

3 Jennens to Handel, 30 August 1745.

4 In the codicil dated 4 August 1757.

5 Burney, 'Sketch', in *An account*, p. 27.

6 Charles Dickens, 'Music in Humble Life' in *Household Words*, vol. 1, p. 163, 11 May 1850. See Andrew Gant, *O Sing Unto the Lord: A History of English Church Music*, Profile, London, 2015, p. 293.

FURTHER READING

This is a small selection of books and other writings which deal specifically with *Messiah*. Notes and introductions to the many editions, recordings and performances also provide an illuminating guide to the work's fascinating (and sometimes wayward) journey through historical time.

Contemporary or near-contemporary sources

Burney, C., *A General History of Music from the Earliest Ages to the Present Period*, four vols, printed for the author, London, 1776–89.

Burney, C., *An Account of the Musical Performances in Westminster-Abbey, and the Pantheon, May 26th, 27th, 29th, and June the 3d and 5th, 1784: In Commemoration of Handel* (1785), T. Payne and Son and G. Robinson, London, 1785.

Mainwaring, J., *Memoirs of the Life of the Late George Frederic Handel: to which is added, a catalogue of his works, and observations upon them*, R. and J. Dodsley, London, 1760.

Modern scholarly works

Burrows, D., *Handel: Messiah*, Cambridge University Press, Cambridge, 1991.

Burrows, D., *Handel and the English Chapel Royal*, Oxford, Oxford University Press, Oxford, 2005.

Keates, J., *Messiah: The Composition and Afterlife of Handel's Masterpiece*, Basic Books, New York, 2017.

Larsen, J.P., *Handel's Messiah: Origins, Composition, Sources*, Greenwood Press, Westport, CT, 1990.

Luckett, R., *Handel's Messiah: A Celebration*, Harcourt Brace, London, 1992.

Shaw, W., *A Textual and Historical Companion to Handel's 'Messiah'*, Novello, London, 1965.

Smith, R., *Handel's Oratorios and Eighteenth-Century Thought*, Cambridge University Press, Cambridge, 1995.

Smith, R., *Charles Jennens: The Man Behind Handel's Messiah*, Handel House Trust, London, 2012.

Tobin, J., *Handel's 'Messiah': A Critical Account of the Manuscript Sources and Printed Editions*, Cassell, London, 1969.

SELECTED DISCOGRAPHY

This personal selection picks out some of the key stages in the work's recorded history.

1899–1920: *A Collector's Messiah*, assembled from a range of live performances. Described as being 'chiefly of historical interest', which is code for 'the performances are unpalatable and the recording virtually inaudible'. But the historical interest is very great indeed – a gathering of bits from some of the very earliest recordings of any music, and a real-time insight into the massed-choir Crystal Palace tradition which took flight soon after Handel's death, and is now largely lost to us. Koch Historic, 3-7703-2Y6 X2.

1927: Sir Thomas Beecham, BBC Symphony Orchestra. The very first (almost) complete recording. Originally on RCA 78s, reissued as Pearl 9456.

1946: Malcolm Sargent, Liverpool Philharmonic Orchestra, Huddersfield Choral Society. Like Beecham, Sargent uses Mozart's orchestration with his own additions. His soloists include the incomparable Isobel Baillie. Columbia 78s, reissued as IMC 220856-304.

1947: Beecham, Royal Philharmonic Orchestra. Beecham's second, with Elsie Suddaby and Heddle Nash among the soloists. Three hours and twenty minutes of *Messiah*. Reissue is Biddulph WHL 059/061.

1959: Beecham, Royal Philharmonic Orchestra. Beecham's third recording, with orchestrations by himself and Eugene Goosens. RCA Victor 09026-61266-2.

1966: Sir Colin Davis, London Symphony Orchestra and Chorus, and a new generation of solo singers including Heather Harper and John Shirley-Quirk. Philips Classics 438 356-2.

1967: Sir Charles Mackerras, English Chamber Orchestra, Ambrosian singers, and soloists Elizabeth Harwood, Janet Baker, Paul Esswood, Robert Tear and Raimund Herincx. A conductor who built historical performance practice and research into his work. EMI Classics 69449.

1972: A conductor who didn't. Cannonball Adderley leads David Axelrod's rock interpretation of *Messiah*. RCA Victor 4636.

1973: Sir David Willcocks, Academy of St Martin-in-the-Fields, Choir of King's College, Cambridge: three of the great names in classical recording, and three more among the adult soloists – James

Bowman, Robert Tear and Benjamin Luxon. One of the first recordings to use boys' voices, including for the soprano solos, as Handel did himself on occasion. EMI Classics, CMS 63784 2.

1976: Sir Neville Marriner, Academy and Chorus of St Martin-in-the-Fields. Typically stylish playing from one of the most reliable names in the recorded library, exploring some of the less often heard variants. London 444824.

1980: Christopher Hogwood, Academy of Ancient Music, Choir of Christ Church Cathedral, Oxford (dir. Simon Preston). One of the first period instrument recordings, with Preston's expert choir. This period also saw the emergence of specialist early music solo singers, including the dazzling young Emma Kirkby. Decca 430 488 2.

1982: John Eliot Gardiner, English Baroque Soloists, Monteverdi Choir. Philips 434297.

1985: Sir Georg Solti, Chicago Symphony Orchestra and chorus, soloists including Kiri te Kanawa. The symphonic approach revisited. London 414 396-2.

1992: *Handel's Messiah: A soulful celebration.* A full-throated big band jazz/gospel version from Quincy Jones. Warner Alliance/World Records 26980.

1993: William Christie, Les Arts Florissants. A stylish 'authentic' reading from an American in Paris and a new generation of soloists. Harmonia Mundi 201498.99.

1999: Andrew Parrott, Handel and Haydn Society. A scholarly recording of the Mozart arrangement. Arabesque 6743.

2006: Edward Higginbottom, Academy of Ancient Music, Choir of New College, Oxford. A recording based on Handel's own performance practice on particular occasions, with boys in the chorus and as soloists. Naxos 8.570131-2.

2009: Stephen Layton, Britten Sinfonia, Polyphony. One of the best of a number of historically informed recordings with expert mixed adult choir and 'modern' orchestra. More than an hour quicker than Beecham in 1947. Hyperion CDA67800.

2013: Emmanuelle Haïm, Le Concert d'Astrée. Solos from established opera singers Christopher Purves and Lucy Crowe. Erato 0825646240555.

2016: Mack Wilberg, Mormon Tabernacle Choir, Orchestra at Temple Square. A reading for large choir which seeks to maintain a baroque aesthetic in a large-scale context. A weighty quartet of soloists adds to the operatic echoes of the massed-choir tradition, including Rolando Villazon and Bryn Terfel. Mormon Tabernacle Choir label, 127902.

PICTURE CREDITS

INDEX